YOUR KEY TO
THE

"By learning the Key Wor... ...could learn to read for others in a matter of days...I have been using this system for 20 years with great success."

—Sylvia Abraham

Sylvia Abraham's unique and easy-to-use Key Word system differs from other systems that use Key Words because it applies to the card numbers of all 78 Tarot cards instead of just the Major Arcana. For example, in the Key Word system, all five number "Two" cards (the Two card of each suit in the Minor Arcana as well as the High Priestess, the Two card of the Major Arcana) have a basic "I KNOW" Key Phrase. These simple Key Phrases are then combined with the symbolic meaning of the four suits to give you a rich source from which to draw your interpretations.

"Sylvia's method is uncannily accurate, yet surprisingly easy to learn. I like the practical information and versatility of the spreads, which can be read on both mundane and esoteric levels."

—Fern Fujimoto

"Sylvia's particular use of universal symbols may surprise some. Her practical application does not concern itself with being 'nice.' Instead, she shares all the perspectives which the symbols can reveal. In handing you a rose, she teaches as well about the thorns, so if you decide to take it, you can realistically hold the stem and still enjoy the bloom."

—Phillip Michaels

HOW TO:

READ THE TAROT

SYLVIA ABRAHAM

2004
Llewellyn Publications
St. Paul, Minnesota 55164-0383, U.S.A.

FIRST EDITION
Tenth printing, 2004
Cover Design: Gavin Dayton Duffy
  Cover image: Adobe Image Library
  Cards on cover from Universal Tarot © Lo Scarabeo.
Used with permission.
Tarot card illustrations reproduced from the designs by
  Pamela Colman Smith in the 1922 reprint of the original
  1910 edition of *The Pictorial Key to the Tarot* by Arthur
  Edward Waite, William Rider & Son Ltd., London

Library of Congress Cataloging-in-Publication Data
Abraham, Sylvia, 1924–
    How to read the tarot / by Abraham, Sylvia.
        p.   cm.
    Includes bibliographical references.
    ISBN 1-56718-001-9
    1. Tarot.   2. Divination   I. Title.
BF1879.T2A37   1994   93-48787
133.2'2424--dc20   CIP

Llewellyn Worldwide does not participate in, endorse, or have any authority or responsibility concerning private business transactions between our authors and the public.

    All mail addressed to the author is forwarded but the publisher cannot, unless specifically instructed by the author, give out an address or phone number.

Llewellyn Publications
A Division of Llewellyn Worldwide, Ltd.
P.O. Box 64383, St. Paul, MN 55164-0383
www.llewellyn.com

Printed in the United States of America

ACKNOWLEDGMENTS

No one ever writes a book alone. I wish to acknowledge my teachers, students, family, and friends who taught me valuable lessons along the way. I am grateful to my family who were supportive in my efforts to gain knowledge regarding the Tarot.

The Rider-Waite Tarot has been the reference for this book. The symbolism of these cards is rich in meaning and is especially good for the beginning student.

CONTENTS

TAROT CARD BEGINNINGS

In ancient times occult studies were taught to those who desired to learn Truth and the meanings of life. These pictures of life were painted or printed on substances such as rock, papyrus, leather, wood, and, more recently, paper. Tarot images were pictured in the pyramids of ancient Egypt, where many secret schools existed. In the past Tarot cards were also used as secret codes, especially during times of strife and unrest.

Through different periods of history, depending on the religious beliefs of the time, occult studies were open to all or taught in the hidden schools. The penalty for disclosure of this knowledge to high officials of the Church was certain death. The mystery schools were in competition with the Church's teachings more often than not. Acquiring an education of any kind during those centuries was possible only through the Church. Many myths and superstitions were projected by the Church in order to control the masses. The Church regulated or denied any information that would enlighten the people.

There are no definite answers concerning when the Tarot was created, only speculation. The Tarot became a pictograph system, putting into art form the meanings of life as it was lived by peasant, artisan, warrior, and king. The fourteenth century has been claimed as the time Tarot cards were first unveiled. It has been stated that the cards began with 22 Major Arcana; that in order to conceal the true meanings of the cards an additional 56 were added (Minor Arcana). It is possible that this statement is true or future evidence may prove it otherwise.

It has been said that the cards were brought to Italy from Spain around the year 1375 A.D. and were introduced by the Moors. Others claim their origin to be Egypt, as Tarot hieroglyphics were found there. The mystery continues!

Regardless of when Tarot cards actually made their appearance, once discovered they became a part of many cultures throughout the world and have been a mainstay in the occult (hidden) lexicon for more than seven centuries. They have withstood the test of time simply because they explain mankind and living conditions universally.

Edward Arthur Waite and Aleister Crowley, both Englishmen and members of the Hermetic Order of the Golden Dawn, were primarily responsible for bringing the Tarot back into popular usage in the early twentieth century. Mr. Waite was a mystic and scholar. His Tarot deck named *The Rider-Waite Tarot* is one of the most widely used in this country. Mr. Crowley was a poet, writer, and student of magic. His Tarot deck, called *The Thoth Tarot,* is also very popular. Others noted for their contribution to Tarot are as follows: Oswald Wirth, Gérard Encausse (*Tarot of the Bohemians*), and Paul Foster Case (*Builders of the Adytum Tarot*). All of these cards have remained in use for many decades because they work.

Open-minded people will search for confirmation regarding all occult studies including Tarot but will not be deterred if it is lacking. Close-minded people fear change and any new information. They prefer to live with old doctrines and worn-out religious beliefs because it is more comfortable.

Tarot cards are more than pretty pictures. They symbolize our unconscious understanding of experience—past, present, and future. The 78 cards represent mankind and all the probable experiences possible to it in life. Tarot cards give information to everyone through archetypal symbols and can stimulate their desire to know more. Perhaps now is the time to use more symbols and less conversation so that we may learn to understand each other in clear and concise ways.

The Tarot has had a resurgence in the past 15 to 20 years. The Tarot cards fall from favor periodically only to be resurrected by those who know the true and deeper meanings behind their symbolism. Some with limited intelligence in the world may seek to extinguish this beautiful tableau only to be thwarted in their attempts.

Those who refuse to accept antiquated answers to eternal questions begin to search for Truth. It is then that they are led to Tarot and other related subjects in the field of metaphysics. Time and energy expended will bring rich rewards to any aspiring student. Whether the student seeks merely a fun way to impress friends, the ability to predict circumstances, or a tool for serious meditation, the results will prove startling! Greater awareness and a new knowledge of the self are just two compensations derived from this ancient work. Tarot cards are a step forward in our evolution to perfection.

TAROT DIVINATION

Through the centuries Tarot cards have been used and abused by readers all over the world. There are those who desire to be "fortunetellers" and many lead their customers astray. The Tarot reader who wishes to impart information and knowledge of a positive nature to a client must hold a positive attitude without judgment.

During the study of Tarot and its symbology, one opens the inner door to intuition. The personal growth attained through this study is apparent to the student. Meditation on the cards awakens the symbology held in the subconscious mind and allows us to realize truth. Our ideas concerning life and the environment have been clothed in materiality. The archetypes held in subconsciousness are ideas of a more spiritual nature. Working with the Tarot opens a passageway between these two areas.

The individual who consults a reader of Tarot feels that the information they receive is absolute truth. In this regard, the reader must always be aware of the responsibility involved. The Tarot is an accurate method of divination. All questions posed to the cards will be answered along with many more insights the client is concerned about.

CHOOSING A TAROT DECK

There are many Tarot decks on the market today and new ones being printed every year. Most Tarot readers do not settle for one deck, but enjoy using different decks depending on the type of reading they intend to give. The different symbols in each deck will clue the mind of the reader into the information they are seeking.

Many different Tarot decks exist at this time. You may want to try the Egyptian, Celtic, Mayan, or Crowley decks—just to mention a few. Study several Tarot decks while you are an apprentice. In the beginning one or two decks may feel more comfortable and the symbols more responsive to your needs. Rest assured that when you have mastered one deck, the rest can be easily understood.

Several decks are compatible with this book such as: the *Robin Wood Tarot*, the *New Golden Dawn*, the *Witches Tarot*, and the Albano-Waite deck. These cards have basic symbols which can be recognized easily. Use the Key Words for each Major Arcana card and test your skills.

The secret of Tarot is in its application. A student of Tarot will soon lose interest in the study if they do not see results. With this book a student can begin to read the cards in three weeks. This can be very exciting. The book is informative and easy to use with most Tarot decks.

The following decks can also be used with some modification: the *Enochian Deck, Temple of Isis,* the *Royal Fez Moroccan Deck,* the *Tarot of the Magicians,* and the *Marseilles* deck. The Major and Minor Arcana of all decks have numbers. Place the four Minor cards of each number next to the Major card of the same number. Familiarize yourself with the symbols of each deck you own. Meditating on the Major Arcana will give you even more information.

The Tarot deck you are currently using will respond to an inner symbology that you understand. Release all tension and allow the symbols to penetrate your subconscious mind. If the Tarot deck which you have purchased does not respond to you—buy another. It does help to feel an affinity for the cards you are using.

There are many modern Tarot decks involved with current trends. Some of them are concerned with crystals, animals, herbs, or Native Americans and new ones being issued constantly. Check for new decks at your favorite store.

READING THE TAROT

When a student begins to read Tarot cards for their family, friends, and self, a certain pattern develops within them. The confidence gained through this study now allows the intuition to flow smoothly. The key words of the Major Arcana click into place and the reading progresses without difficulty. The information presented to the client has the potential to change that person's life completely.

At the beginning, the reader should engage the client in conversation regarding the question or purpose of the reading. There should be a friendly exchange between the reader and client to put them at ease. If the reading is for fun, not profit, there will be less tension and more camaraderie. If the reading is for profit, the reader (if not experienced) may become overanxious and shut off any psychic exchange between the two. The more relaxed the reader and client are, the clearer and more comprehensive the reading.

Tarot readings can be exhausting, using up time and energy. When a reader becomes confident of their skill, charging a fee is quite proper. Human beings have a tendency to respect what they pay for. In that vein, readings will have a value and be taken more seriously. This does place a heavy responsibility on the reader. The ethical reader will not lead a client on a false trail nor embellish the truth. This type of negativity leads to Karmic experiences for the reader such as "as you sow, so shall you reap."

Many of my students have become professional Tarot readers. Most of them continue with their studies in the fields of astrology, numerology, palmistry, and metaphysics. Knowledge of these other fields enhances the Tarot reading by giving additional information to the client. To get the best reading, use a spread you are comfortable with, a Tarot deck you understand, and read for a client who really needs help and is willing to listen to the oracle of Tarot.

THE TAROT DECK

A Tarot deck has 78 cards which are broken down in the following manner:

- 22 Major Arcana

- 40 Minor Arcana

- 16 Court Cards

The word "arcana" means secret or hidden. The Major Arcana are "big secrets." The Minor Arcana are "little secrets."

The <u>Major Arcana cards reveal the character and mental condition of the Querent</u> (person getting the reading). These cards are the most important in the spread. The Major Arcana cards can be used alone and will answer whatever questions are asked of them.

The <u>Minor Arcana cards show specific directions in the person's life and thinking and explain ideas, people at work or home, and others in relationships.</u> The Minor Arcana has four suits: Wands, Cups, Pentacles, and Swords. The explanations on the next page give key words and descriptions of each suit.

WANDS

Key Words: Work and social activities
Element of Fire: Action, enthusiasm, courage, zeal, passion, enterprise
Zodiacal Signs: Aries, Leo, Sagittarius

CUPS

Key Words: Love and emotions
Element of Water: Emotions, intuition, subconscious, memories, birth, marriage
Zodiacal Signs: Cancer, Scorpio, Pisces

PENTACLES

Key Words: Money and health
Element of Earth: Stability, dependability, reliability, material possessions, health matters
Zodiacal Signs: Taurus, Virgo, Capricorn

SWORDS

Key Words: Problems and troubles
Element of Air: Mental attitudes, discrimination, strife, adaptability
Zodiacal Signs: Gemini, Libra, Aquarius

In a spread:

- *Many Wands:* Work or social activities

- *Many Cups:* Love or emotional matters

- *Many Pentacles:* Money matters or health problems

- *Many Swords:* Problems or troubles

- *Many Major Arcana and Court Cards:* Too many people are trying to influence the Querent

The cards are described on the following pages, memorize the key words for each suit and each number. If a Major Arcana card is not in the spread but a Minor Arcana card of that same numerical series is, the key phrase of the Major Arcana card applies.

Example: 2 of Wands
The key phrase of the High Priestess, Key 2, is: "I know." Every card marked number 2 in the Minor Arcana also refers to the phrase "I know." So the 2 of Wands is: *I know my work and social activities.*

Example: 4 of Cups
The key phrase of the Emperor, Key 4, is: "I realize." Every card marked number 4 in the Minor Arcana also refers to the phrase "I realize." So the 4 of Cups is: *I realize my love and emotions, but I am still thinking about past loves.*

Example: 3 of Pentacles
The key phrase of the Empress, Key 3, is: "I make." Every card marked number 3 in the Minor Arcana refers to the phrase "I make." So the 3 of Pentacles is: *I make money because I am a master craftsman and do my job well.*

Example: 6 of Swords
The key phrase of the Lovers, Key 6, is: "I choose." All Minor Arcana cards marked number 6 refer to the phrase "I choose." So the 6 of Swords is: *I choose to stay or run away from my problems and troubles.*

THE FOOL.

final outcome — 1st reading

0 THE FOOL

someone on their way to something

Key Word: Everyone   *Minor Arcana:* None

Ruled by: Uranus   *Element:* Air

Positive Attributes: Freedom, Joy, Happiness, Youth, New experiences, Inexperience, Adventure

Negative Attributes: Foolish desires, Selfishness, Ignorance, Irresponsibility, Unwise actions, Pleasure seeker, Sexual focus

The Fool is humanity on its way to experience. The wand he carries is a phallic symbol. Within his pouch are all the tools necessary for leading a successful life. The rose is the flower of Venus, planet of love and desire. The white rose he carries signifies pure love. A dog is considered man's best friend and this one is trying to caution the Fool to be careful of his steps. The dog also refers to our animal nature and our five senses. The snow in the distance shows us that the world can be a cold place in which to live and also refers to frozen mental attitudes. The white Sun behind the Fool is our true source of life, the super-consciousness.

Uranus rules Aquarius, an air sign. It refers to mental activity. Qualities of Uranus are: desire for new experiences, adventure, friendships, new age thinking, invention, and sudden events.

Fool Upright in a Spread

This indicates a desire for new experiences, sudden activity, and adventure. There is a need for caution at this time, a misstep can send one over the edge. Pay attention to the environment and use insight through all circumstances. Be confident, but do not act hastily.

Fool Reversed in a Spread

Confidence is lacking. There is a need to take more responsibility. Balance pleasures, sexual needs, and other desires. Curb anxiety, have faith in the future. Other possibilities include: immature thinking and actions, selfishness, materialistic focus, or an unkind friend.

I THE MAGICIAN

Key Words: I will   *Minor Arcana:* Aces

Ruled by: Mercury   *Element:* Air

Positive Attributes: New beginnings, Understanding, Meditation, Mental growth, Desire, Leadership, Originality, Awareness

Negative Attributes: Stagnation, Imbalance, Boredom, Lacks self-confidence, Closed mind, Incompetent, Physical drives, Egotistical nature

The Magician is self-conscious awareness. He understands "As Above, So Below." The Magician must balance his desires and passions in order to have a better life. Meditation is vital to his growth. The wand is a phallic symbol which he must learn to control through his mind. The garden refers to the vegetable kingdom as do the roses, lilies, and the greenery. The roses symbolize desire and the five senses; the white lilies symbolize knowledge and purity.

Mercury, an air planet, rules both Gemini (an air sign) and Virgo (an earth sign). Mercury is called the "Messenger of the Gods!" He is swift and changeable.

THE MAGICIAN

My Concern #1 reading

MAGICIAN UPRIGHT IN A SPREAD
<u>I will have new beginnings in many directions of my life.</u> Leadership potential, ambition, desire for activity, and <u>new relationships.</u> Life is eternal. <u>New lessons to learn. Pay attention to details,</u> Growth in the mental body as well as the physical. Meditate on the tools at your disposal for a new experience.

MAGICIAN REVERSED IN A SPREAD
I will not have any new beginnings in areas of my desires. Lack of ambition or drive. Static behavior. Feeling put down, low self-esteem. Creativity arrested. Physical and sexual focus. Ignoring responsibilities. Being closed to new information.

ACE of WANDS.

ACE OF WANDS

ACE OF WANDS UPRIGHT IN A SPREAD

I will have new beginnings in work and social activities. New thinking in business, new opportunities, and new contacts socially. Excitement due to new interests. Beginning a new job.

ACE OF WANDS REVERSED IN A SPREAD

I will not have new beginnings in work or socially. Postponements, trips deferred, and plans canceled. Depression. Little happiness. End of relations in work or socially. No growth.

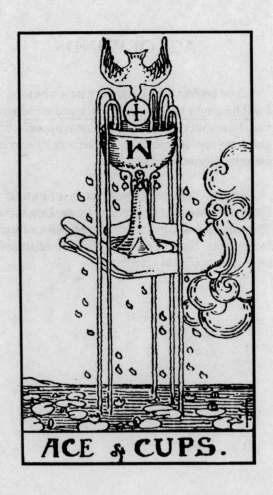

ACE ᛦ CUPS.

ACE OF CUPS

ACE OF CUPS UPRIGHT IN A SPREAD

I will have new beginnings in love relationships. New residence, happiness, and pleasure. Emotionally upbeat. Peace and balance in life. Good health. Trust intuition now. Good news.

ACE OF CUPS REVERSED IN A SPREAD

I will not have new beginnings in love. Emotional instability. Loss or separation. Feeling drained. Lack of inner trust. Upsetting news. Stagnation. Quarrels with friends.

ACE of PENTACLES

ACE OF PENTACLES

ACE OF PENTACLES UPRIGHT IN A SPREAD
I will have new beginnings with money. Prosperity.
New offers involving money. Inheritance or winning
through a gamble. Relationship based on financial
security. Improved health conditions. Happiness.

ACE OF PENTACLES REVERSED IN A SPREAD
No new beginnings with money. Financial picture
gloomy. Greed and jealousy can affect the health in
negative ways. Learn to balance the budget. Don't
borrow money at this time. Conserve resources.

ACE of SWORDS.

ACE OF SWORDS

ACE OF SWORDS UPRIGHT IN A SPREAD

I will have new beginnings in problems and troubles. Old problems are ending making way for new ones. A need to release negative mental attitudes. A loss of family or friend. Potential for an operation or cutting off some experience. New events now.

ACE OF SWORDS REVERSED IN A SPREAD

I will not have new beginnings in problems or troubles. I need to resolve the ones I have now. Lack of mental perception. Little self-confidence. Fear of the future. Boredom. No new ideas regarding changes in my life.

THE HIGH PRIESTESS

II THE HIGH PRIESTESS

Key Words: I know   *Minor Arcana:* Twos

Ruled by: Moon   *Element:* Water

Positive Attributes: Science, Reason, Good intellect, Memory, Knowledge, Secret wisdom, Emotions, Subconscious, Intuition

Negative Attributes: Closed mind, Egotistical, Over-emotional, Superficial, Unskilled, Selfish, Duality, Fearful, Illusion

The High Priestess is a repository for secret wisdom. The symbol of the Moon tells of the danger of releasing higher knowledge to unprepared minds. The High Priestess sits at the doorway of the temple (body) ready and willing to allow entrance to all aspiring students. The water flowing at her feet runs through the entire series of Tarot cards. The Moon and water refer to subconsciousness, the female, intuition, and the color blue. The scroll she holds in her hand is the memory we all carry within us of our past, present, and future called Akasha. She sits between two pillars—Jachin and Boaz indicating the duality of all life. The cross on the High Priestess shows a balance of the four elements—fire, air, water, and earth. The pomegranates symbolize the seeds of life (female); the fronds symbolize pointed greenery (male).

Moon rules Cancer, fourth sign of the zodiac. The Moon is water. The Moon indicates the emotions, memory, mother, and the home.

THE HIGH PRIESTESS

HIGH PRIESTESS UPRIGHT IN A SPREAD

I know the secrets of the universe. Intelligent comprehension of all nature. Scientific and mathematical knowledge. Nurturing and caring for others. Desire for a sharing relationship. Self-confident attitude. In a man's spread it represents a desire for an intelligent mate. Trust intuition. Use information wisely.

HIGH PRIESTESS REVERSED IN A SPREAD

I don't know the meaning of life or how to make a good relationship. Fixed mental attitude. Fear of commitment. Emotionally drained. Intuitive abilities ignored. Critical or overanalytical. Information taken at face value denoting superficiality. Illusion.

TWO OF WANDS

TWO OF WANDS UPRIGHT IN A SPREAD
I know my work and social activities. I have the world in my hands and can be successful. I use my knowledge in social interaction and in business. I desire balance in both areas of life. Using will and ego in work and socially.

TWO OF WANDS REVERSED IN A SPREAD
I don't know my work or my place in society. Unbalanced actions at work or in relationships with others. Business know-how lacking. Little confidence in abilities or skills. Fear of failure. Too critical and little ambition.

TWO OF CUPS

TWO OF CUPS UPRIGHT IN A SPREAD
I know about love and emotions. I know a good relationship is emotionally healthy. Potential for an engagement, marriage, or birth announcement. Happy events. Plans for the future. Trusting intuition.

TWO OF CUPS REVERSED IN A SPREAD
I know nothing about love. Health affected due to unhappy emotions. Sexual incompatibility. Superficial love never lasts. Loss or separation creates an emotional drain. Unbalanced emotions. Divorce.

TWO OF PENTACLES

TWO OF PENTACLES UPRIGHT IN A SPREAD
I know how to balance my money. Financial gain through others. Balancing money and health is an eternal struggle. Desire for material possessions. Faith in future prosperity. Good health conditions.

TWO OF PENTACLES REVERSED IN A SPREAD
I don't know how to handle money. Depression over financial affairs. Money loss. Poverty minded. Health problems due to money conditions. Earning capacity limited through lack of skills. Materialistic.

TWO OF SWORDS

Two of Swords Upright in a Spread

I know my problems and troubles but I don't want to see them. Refusing to face the problems which can be dangerous. Going within for answers. Inner understanding. Passive attitude but may need to take action. Intuition may not be clear.

Two of Swords Reversed in a Spread

I don't know my problems or troubles; I don't want to face them either. Illusory thinking. Situation may not be as hopeless as it seems. Not willing to use intuition or trust inner resources. Fear of new knowledge. Physical focus not mental.

THE EMPRESS.

III THE EMPRESS

Key Words: I make   *Minor Arcana:* Threes

Ruled by: Venus   *Elements:* Earth and Air

Positive Attributes: Mother Nature, Creativity, Marriage, Union, Pregnancy, Communication, Imagination, Pleasure, Sexuality

Negative Attributes: Unhappiness, Infertility, Mental problems, Unloving, Selfish, Dull, Lack of growth, Lacking talent

The Empress is Mother Nature at work bringing us life and all good things in abundance. She is Venus, the planet of loving and giving. The Empress is pregnant and promises us a harvest in the future. She is in pursuit of pleasure, sex, creativity, and union. She is the mother of all and cares for all her children equally. Her shield is love and her scepter is a symbol of Venus. The crown on her head shows her authority. Her color is green referring to love and growth.

Venus rules Taurus and Libra, the second and seventh signs of the zodiac. Taurus is an earth sign; Libra is an air sign. Venus is the planet of love, beauty, desires, and pleasure.

THE EMPRESS.

THE EMPRESS UPRIGHT IN A SPREAD

I make or create my experiences. Potential for pregnancy. The focus is on happiness, travel, and enjoyment. A need to communicate desires now. Issues relating to mother, sisters or other females important. Time to use creative talents. A very positive growth period. Put intuition to good use. An authority figure who is gentle and caring.

THE EMPRESS REVERSED IN A SPREAD

I don't make or create my experiences. Problems with mother and or other females. Miscarriage, sexually unfulfilled. I don't make myself happy, bring love into my life, or feel confident about my creative talents. Lost relationship. Mental anguish. Trips delayed. Inability to communicate true feelings.

THREE OF WANDS

THREE OF WANDS UPRIGHT IN A SPREAD

I make my work and social activities. Potential for partnership. Desire to create a new business or make a new relationship. Seeking inner guidance for future plans in work or socially. New ideas bring success and happiness. Creative growth.

THREE OF WANDS REVERSED IN A SPREAD

I don't make my work or have a happy creative social life. Lacking faith in personal talents. No commitment in the work or to a relationship. Communication skills ineffective. Inner guidance ignored. Little growth or balance in life. Vision faulty.

THREE OF CUPS

THREE OF CUPS UPRIGHT IN A SPREAD

I make myself happy doing the things I love. Good times with friends. Emotional upbeat. Making plans for a celebration including: marriage, engagement, birth, or travel. A sexual period, pregnancy, or creativity through the arts, music and literature. Joy.

THREE OF CUPS REVERSED IN A SPREAD

I don't make myself happy in love. Having difficulties in a love relationship. An emotional drain, some depression, and/or loss. Potential for miscarriage or abortion. Overindulgence. Friendship at an end. Problems with liquor or drugs. Loneliness.

THREE OF PENTACLES

THREE OF PENTACLES UPRIGHT IN A SPREAD
I make my money. I am a master craftsman, good at what I do. Creative talents bring financial rewards. Communications regarding money and health. Success through faith in my abilities.

THREE OF PENTACLES REVERSED IN A SPREAD
I don't make money. Feeling overqualified or unskilled in my work. Lacking faith or trust in creative abilities. Unhappy with personal finances. Money concerns can affect the health. Materialism.

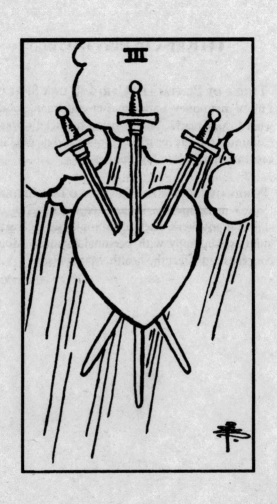

THREE OF SWORDS

THREE OF SWORDS UPRIGHT IN A SPREAD

I make my own problems and troubles. A love triangle or feeling betrayed. Shedding tears. Lawsuit through separation or divorce. Conflicts can lead to accidents. Health problems can indicate an operation. Cheating. Incompatibility.

THREE OF SWORDS REVERSED IN A SPREAD

I don't make my problems or troubles. A rival. Unhappiness in a love relationship. Feeling stabbed in the back. Deceit. A friend proves untrustworthy. Mental confusion. Affairs of the heart create health problems.

THE EMPEROR.

IV THE EMPEROR

Key Words: I Realize   *Minor Arcana:* Fours

Ruled by: Aries   *Element:* Fire

Positive Attributes: Balance, Stability, Leadership, Authority, Father image, Knowledge, Action, Power, Truth

Negative Attributes: Lacks authority, Immaturity, Inexperience, Impulsive, Unstable, Untruthful, Vacillation, Inertia

The Emperor is a symbol of balanced mental activity. He is experience and authority by virtue of his age and position. The Emperor is wisdom and kindness shown by his passive attitude (seated), but he is dressed for action (armor). He is the father figure in whom we put our trust and hopes. Aries rules here and indicates the will and ego held in check through realization. The throne on which he is seated gives him the right to be ruler. The Egyptian ankh held in the Emperor's right hand is a symbol of love and immortality. The color blue, from the High Priestess, implies he has intuitive understanding.

Aries is the first sign of the zodiac. Aries rules the head (mental). It is the sign of: leadership, initiative, action, energy, and new ideas.

THE EMPEROR.

THE EMPEROR UPRIGHT IN A SPREAD

Desire for balance, realization, and action. Ability to use authority wisely. Leadership qualities tempered with love. Benevolence. Real estate buying or selling. Home issues resolved. Mental abilities used before action taken. Seeking truth through experience. A wise and gentle counselor. Ambition with the energy to accomplish goals.

THE EMPEROR REVERSED IN A SPREAD

Not realizing potential, being fearful and immature. Refusing to accept leadership roles due to inexperience or laziness. Egotistical and arrogant. Ruthless actions and little follow-through in many areas of life. Sexual needs too important. Juvenile mentality. Dishonesty. Instability. Materialistic.

FOUR OF WANDS

FOUR OF WANDS UPRIGHT IN A SPREAD

I realize my need for work and social activities. Stable business methods and happy social encounters. Fruitfulness and endurance. Marriage. Buying or selling real estate. Achievement and harmony.

FOUR OF WANDS REVERSED IN A SPREAD

I don't realize my imbalance in work or in my social life. Loss of prosperity. Business activity declining. Extravagance depletes financial assets. Separation or divorce. Immature actions. Egoism.

FOUR OF CUPS

FOUR OF CUPS UPRIGHT IN A SPREAD

I realize my love and emotions. The focus is on past love experiences which may not be positive. Be aware of a new love relationship potential. Overcome depression with a new mental attitude. Old habit patterns must be released. A need for sexual balance.

FOUR OF CUPS REVERSED IN A SPREAD

I am not realizing my love and emotional drain. An unhappy love affair. Disappointed in a love or sexual relationship. Fear of commitment or rejection. Boredom. Separation or loss. Inexperienced in relationships. Unrealistic expectations.

FOUR OF PENTACLES

FOUR OF PENTACLES UPRIGHT IN A SPREAD
I realize my money and the value of material possessions. Avarice. Buying or selling property. Keep a balanced attitude about money—don't idolize it. Inheritance. Good health. The Midas touch.

FOUR OF PENTACLES REVERSED IN A SPREAD
I don't realize the value of money. Setback in finances. Gambling. Spendthrift. A need to balance your budget. Health adversely affected by financial problems. Inexperienced in money matters. Property values deflated.

FOUR OF SWORDS

FOUR OF SWORDS UPRIGHT IN A SPREAD

I realize my problems and troubles. Rest from strife. Having the faith to overcome mental struggles. Retreat, rest, and recover. Seeking help from inner sources. Overindulgences must be halted. Health needs must be recognized now.

FOUR OF SWORDS REVERSED IN A SPREAD

I don't realize my problems and troubles. Anxiety and nervous tension. Burning the candle at both ends creates physical problems. Lacking faith. Sexual desires are the focus. Immature actions.

THE HIEROPHANT

V THE HIEROPHANT

Key Words: I Believe   *Minor Arcana:* Fives

Ruled by: Taurus   *Element:* Earth

Positive Attributes: Inner Teacher/Guide, Karma, Intuition, Psychic ability, Discipline, Social approval, Minor changes, Meditation

Negative Attributes: Intolerance, Dogma, Inertia, Boredom, Self doubt, Materialistic, No changes, Fear

The Hierophant is the Inner Teacher. By quieting ourselves through meditation we listen to that "still small voice" and are guided, giving us more faith in life. Through this method we can overcome all negative experiences and become one with our inner source. The Hierophant holds a scepter that symbolizes the three worlds—physical, astral, and etheric. His right hand is held up to give blessings to all. The ministers at his feet represent reverence, wisdom and understanding. The pillars, shown previously in Key II, the High Priestess, indicate the duality in the world. The two Keys are gold (male) and silver (female). The yoke on the Hierophant and the two ministers refer to the Path and yoga.

Taurus, second sign of the zodiac. Taurus is an earth sign. Material symbol of pleasure, enjoyment, self-worth and the senses. Taurus is ruled by the planet Venus—love and creativity.

V

THE HIEROPHANT

THE HIEROPHANT UPRIGHT IN A SPREAD

Desire for a teacher. Needing help to overcome problems. Time to meditate, be silent and trust intuition. Karmic conditions must be resolved. Longing for approval. Resenting authority or control by others. Faith in the Higher Self brings positive results. Inner listening. Small changes available at this time. Investigate motivations in all experiences.

THE HIEROPHANT REVERSED IN A SPREAD

Pleasure seeker, indulgent and materialistic. Dissipation. Lacks faith in self or a higher source. Fears change. Intolerant and judgmental views. Refusing to accept new information. Sexual focus and physical gratification important now. Unused creative talents.

FIVE OF WANDS

FIVE OF WANDS UPRIGHT IN A SPREAD

I believe in work and social activities. I believe in my ideas, will, and ego over others. Desire for a change in work conditions. Many challenges from coworkers. Family strife. Discord and disharmony.

FIVE OF WANDS REVERSED IN A SPREAD

I don't believe in my ideas in the work or socially. Fear of disharmony in relationships personally or at work. Little faith in self or abilities. Self-confidence lacking and low self-esteem. Legal problems.

FIVE OF CUPS

FIVE OF CUPS UPRIGHT IN A SPREAD
I believe in love. False love brings emotional discontent. Ignorance in love relations. Crying over spilled milk. Broken marriage or romance. Desire for sex and pleasure. Liquor or drug problems. A fickle lover. Memories of a lost love still hurt.

FIVE OF CUPS REVERSED IN A SPREAD
I don't believe in love or romance. An emotional drain regarding family or loved ones. Unbalanced emotions, fear of the future, and little trust in a relationship. Divorce or separation. Frustration.

FIVE OF PENTACLES

FIVE OF PENTACLES UPRIGHT IN A SPREAD

I believe in money, it is my god. Belief in money can be crippling. Unemployment card. Lack of faith in self and creative talents. Poverty-minded. Health issues must be checked. Feeling unsupported. Drugs. Use prosperity as a mantra.

FIVE OF PENTACLES REVERSED IN A SPREAD

I don't believe in money as my god. A new job or work that can be difficult. Beginnings of faith in own talents and self. No changes create fear and depression. Take care of health. Get in touch with your inner guide for direction.

FIVE OF SWORDS

FIVE OF SWORDS UPRIGHT IN A SPREAD
I believe in problems and troubles. A desire to overcome others due to ego needs. Empty victory. Loss of friends through cruel actions. Unhealthy mental attitude. Rash behavior. Changes may not be positive now. Desires cloud good sense in relations.

FIVE OF SWORDS REVERSED IN A SPREAD
I don't believe in problems and troubles. Peaceful relationships. No desire to beat others for ego gratification. Seeking mental balance and harmonious changes. Negative thoughts not acted upon.

THE LOVERS.

VI THE LOVERS

Key Words: I Choose   *Minor Arcana:* Sixes

Ruled by: Gemini   *Element:* Air

Positive Attributes: Making decisions, Higher mind, Responsibility, Honesty, Marriage, Faith, Attraction

Negative Attributes: Indecision, Frustration, Irresponsibility, Dishonesty, Infidelity, Sexual drive, Hedonistic

The Lovers card refers to discrimination, making right choices and having faith. The male and female principles are looking to the Higher Self for guidance. The Tree of Life stands behind the male and holds 12 fruits (signs of the zodiac). The Tree of Knowledge of good and evil stands behind the female and indicates our divided mind and feelings of separation from our source. The two figures represent Adam and Eve in the garden of Eden and the temptations before us. The pyramid is a symbol of physical manifestation and reminds us of our ability to reach high for attainment. This card also indicates the marriage of our dual natures. The archangel is Raphael, God as Healer. The serpent depicts the kundalini force going up the spine and bringing enlightenment. The serpent is also wisdom and temptation.

Gemini is the third sign of the zodiac, an air sign (mental), and rules over: siblings, neighbors, lower mind, versatility, literature, teaching, and short trips.

THE LOVERS.

THE LOVERS UPRIGHT IN A SPREAD

Making a choice between vice and virtue. Using discrimination in all experiences. Seeking answers from the Higher Self and having faith that help will be forthcoming. Accepting responsibilities for all actions. Controlling desires, being in harmony with others. Be aware of subconscious habit patterns repeating themselves. Make decisions now. No time for marriage. Make plans for a trip, social event or taking care of health matters.

THE LOVERS REVERSED IN A SPREAD

Not making choices. Engagement or marriage plans delayed. Apprehensive about making decisions, fear of being wrong. Lack of trust in self or inner self. Superficial. Sexual indulgences. Infidelity. Potential for health problems. Closed minded. Irresponsible actions. Dishonest in relationships.

SIX OF WANDS

SIX OF WANDS UPRIGHT IN A SPREAD

I choose my work and social activities. Making right decisions regarding work and in my social life. Victory. Balanced ego needs. Control of the senses. Right use of will and energy.

SIX OF WANDS REVERSED IN A SPREAD

Making unwise choices. Negative use of energy and will in work and social activities. Temptations overcome common sense. Delays at work. No victory. Avoid setbacks by right action and thought. Seek help from within.

SIX OF CUPS

SIX OF CUPS UPRIGHT IN A SPREAD

Making intelligent choices in love relations. Happy emotional affairs. Temptation to live in the past, not in the present. Friend or lover from the past. Responsibilities in family matters. Gift from an admirer. Desire for new love affair or marriage.

SIX OF CUPS REVERSED IN A SPREAD

Not making choices creates an emotional drain. Indecision in love/marriage. Irresponsible actions in relationships. Loss, separation, or divorce. Illness through stressful events. Lack of growth or harmony.

SIX OF PENTACLES

SIX OF PENTACLES UPRIGHT IN A SPREAD
I make choices with my money. Learning to be fair and sharing with resources. Balanced finances make life happier and healthy. I am choosing new ways to create money. Helping the less fortunate.

SIX OF PENTACLES REVERSED IN A SPREAD
I don't make choices about money. Not charitable or sharing. Unwise decisions in financial matters. Poverty minded. Health problems due to fear of material lack. Spendthrift. Selfish with resources.

VI

SIX OF SWORDS

SIX OF SWORDS UPRIGHT IN A SPREAD

Making choices regarding my problems and troubles. The temptation is to run away or stay and face the music (problems and troubles). Unhealthy relationship. Lack of knowledge or realization brings problems to you. Taking a trip over water (or near water). Mental strain. Seek help within.

SIX OF SWORDS REVERSED IN A SPREAD

I don't make choices about my problems and troubles. I must stay and face the situation. Having difficulty coping with the problems. Depression. Lack of faith. Plans delayed. Don't allow others to make your decisions. Attend to health matters.

THE CHARIOT.

VII THE CHARIOT

Key Words: The Path   *Minor Arcana:* Sevens

Ruled by: Cancer   *Element:* Water

Positive Attributes: Success, Mental control, Security, Inner guidance, Area of activity, Cycles, Confidence

Negative Attributes: Overconfidence, Materialism, Lack of knowledge, Unstable forces, Prejudice, Lack of Direction, Superstition

The Chariot is the physical vehicle (the body) which must be mentally directed. There are no reins to guide the senses (sphinxes). This implies that each person must use control with their mind over all experiences in their lives. The wheels of the Chariot signify cycles and indicate changes. The Moons (on the shoulders of the Charioteer) refer to subconscious emotions and old habit patterns of thinking which must be transformed. The white and black sphinxes are a blend of self-consciousness, subconsciousness, masculine, and feminine energies. Mental awareness is the arena of experience referred to by Key 7. The belt and skirt on the Charioteer show time and the zodiac.

Cancer, a water sign, is the fourth sign of the zodiac and refers to: home, mother, real estate, sympathy, nurturing, and tenacity.

THE CHARIOT.

THE CHARIOT UPRIGHT IN A SPREAD

Now is the time to use mental powers to control destiny and be victorious. Direct your energies on the path (mental) then take action. The Charioteer is your Higher Self, trust Him to guide you in all your affairs. Know what you want first. Life is cyclic and the wheels turn slowly. Use sexual energy wisely. Take a trip.

THE CHARIOT REVERSED IN A SPREAD

Unwise direction of energy. Moderation is a must at all times. Lack of trust in inner guidance makes life difficult. Use care with liquor/drugs. Self-indulgence. Snobbery. Imprisonment. Opinionated. A need for mental clarity.

SEVEN OF WANDS

SEVEN OF WANDS UPRIGHT IN A SPREAD

Taking the mental path in work and social activities. Success and victory in business. Rely on own judgment. Selective in social matters. Feeling superior at work. Desire to express own ego and will in the marketplace. New ideas. Mental control.

SEVEN OF WANDS REVERSED IN A SPREAD

No victory in business or socially. Feeling inferior or incompetent at work. Physical and material desires are the focus. No mental control. Path unclear for the future. Take care with liquor/drugs. Ego needs not being met. No changes at this time.

SEVEN OF CUPS

Seven of Cups Upright in a Spread
Victory gained in love. Path of creative visualization or daydreaming. Mental control over emotions brings balance. Desire for material happiness or spiritual attainment. Seek guidance from within. Liquor and drugs add to the illusion—remove the rose colored glasses.

Seven of Cups Reversed in a Spread
Defeat through love and emotional needs. Loss or separation creates an emotional drain. Little faith or trust in inner resources. Physical path more important than using mental abilities. Lacking control over the senses. Anger/jealousy can ruin health.

SEVEN OF PENTACLES

SEVEN OF PENTACLES UPRIGHT IN A SPREAD

The path to money brings victory. Mental focus is on financial responsibilities. A wish to use money wisely. Prosperity minded. Maintaining health and well being through feelings of security. Ego confidence and stability with money.

SEVEN OF PENTACLES REVERSED IN A SPREAD

Uncertain path to money. Success not assured—no money tree. Health afflicted through material loss. A lack of confidence in self. Frustration and anxiety. Insecurity and paranoia. Little money sense. No inner faith. Pettiness and jealousy.

SEVEN OF SWORDS

SEVEN OF SWORDS UPRIGHT IN A SPREAD
Taking a path to problems and troubles. The situation is temporary. Mentally creating problems in relationships. Feeling cheated or loss of valuables. Danger through travel or sports. Desire for new experiences but not in an honest way. Pay attention.

SEVEN OF SWORDS REVERSED IN A SPREAD
No victory with my problems and troubles. The situation is stagnate. Jealousy over others' success. Mental ideas are directed to physical and material desires. Unhappy relationship that seems permanent. No faith or trust in self.

VIII

STRENGTH.

VIII STRENGTH

Key Word: Strength **Minor Arcana:** Eights

Ruled by: Leo **Element:** Fire

Positive Attributes: Energy, Courage, Overcoming temptation, Mental growth, Attraction/Repulsion, Fortitude, Power

Negative Attributes: Egotism, Lack of energy, Ruthlessness, Physical focus, Little faith, Deceit/Conceit, Cowardice, Gambling

The Strength card refers to the eternal struggle to overcome the animalistic passions within each of us. The lion (Leo, the ego) rages inside our bodies and desires to be heard. The female (subconsciousness) must subdue these tendencies. She has the courage. She is seen here putting her hands around the lion's mouth. We must all have the strength to control our passions and desires so that we may continue our evolutionary growth. The wreath, symbol of victory, entwines the female and the red lion, revealing that harmony can be maintained between them. The lemniscate (figure 8 over female's head) is the sign of eternity. The greenery over her head indicates mental growth.

Leo, a fire sign, is the fifth sign of the zodiac. It refers to energy, action, and initiative and is the sign of the ego, creative talents, gambling, generosity, and is fun loving.

STRENGTH UPRIGHT IN A SPREAD

We have the strength to overcome all difficulties. Courage and endurance. Leadership qualities. Person has the ability to win over any adversity. Learning to control passions and desires. A true friend. Strength to resist temptations. Artistic talents should be investigated. A need for ego recognition. Sexual balance.

STRENGTH REVERSED IN A SPREAD

Lacking the strength to overcome difficulties in life. Little self-control. Egotistical, loud, and vain. Lazy or overly ambitious. Limited knowledge regarding inner resources. Active sexual life. Not a trustworthy friend due to jealousy or dishonesty. A follower, not a leader. Ruthless in positions of power.

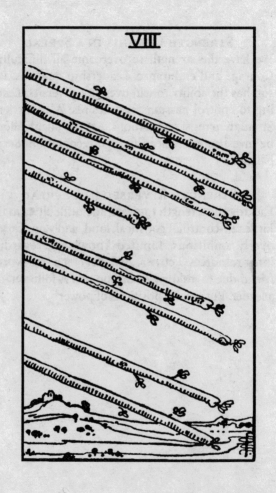

EIGHT OF WANDS

EIGHT OF WANDS UPRIGHT IN A SPREAD

I have the strength to do the work and be involved in an active social life. Balanced plans in business. Overcoming obstacles in work and also socially. Traveling for business and or pleasure. Messages regarding work. Self-confidence and ambition.

EIGHT OF WANDS REVERSED IN A SPREAD

Lacking strength in work or social activities. Delays create frustration on the job or in my social life. No messages or travel plans now. Insecurity. Unbalanced thoughts or actions can bring failure in the work or in a relationship. Health can suffer.

EIGHT OF CUPS

EIGHT OF CUPS UPRIGHT IN A SPREAD

I have strength in my love and emotions. Overcoming temptations and desires. Searching for spiritual meaning. Sensing danger in too much physical activity. Letting go of past emotional experiences. Trusting intuition. Travel plans are working out. Changing attitudes regarding love and relationships.

EIGHT OF CUPS REVERSED IN A SPREAD

Lacking strength in love or emotions. An emotional drain due to loss, separation, or other negative events. Health problems resulting from unbalanced emotions. Physical and sexual drives lead to frustration. Conceit and egotism. Refusing to see the danger of an overactive libido.

EIGHT OF PENTACLES

EIGHT OF PENTACLES UPRIGHT IN A SPREAD

Having the strength and persistence to earn money. The apprentice. Learning new skills. Perseverance in work brings financial rewards. Using inner strength to create a new image and ego. Gaining confidence and self-esteem. Ambition.

EIGHT OF PENTACLES REVERSED IN A SPREAD

Not having the strength to make money or spend time learning new skills. Dislike of hard work. Desire for quick money. Criminal activities. Little responsibility with money and a lack of confidence. Lazy.

EIGHT OF SWORDS

EIGHT OF SWORDS UPRIGHT IN A SPREAD

Having the strength to cope with problems and troubles. In bondage. On unsafe ground. Troubles in relationships. Potential health problems. Fear of making changes. Loss or separation. Look within for answers.

EIGHT OF SWORDS REVERSED IN A SPREAD

Lacking the strength to handle problems and troubles. Feeling unsafe in the midst of chaos. Mental unhappiness. Let go of unhealthy situations or suffer the consequences. Little confidence or faith in self.

THE HERMIT.

IX THE HERMIT

Key Words: Wisdom Through Experience   *Minor Arcana:* Nines

Ruled by: Virgo   *Element:* Earth

Positive Attributes: Knowledge, Guidance, Study, Aloneness, Wisdom, Experience, Insight, Spiritual Quest

Negative Attributes: Immaturity, Prejudice, Inexperienced, Unreasonable, Uninspired, Not enlightened, Health issues, Dogmatic

The Hermit holds his lantern aloft to show us the way to attainment. The two interlocking triangles symbolize the four elements, fire, earth, air, and water in harmony. The Hermit is ancient, indicating wisdom, authority, maturity, and judgment. He has had many experiences in living and now desires to share his information with us. The Hermit is our inner teacher and guide whom we contact through meditation. The gray of his beard and cloak are symbols of the masculine and feminine elements blended. The six-pointed star is the Star of David. David in the Bible refers to the "beloved of God." The staff (phallic symbol) is held in the left hand (subconsciousness). The Hermit stands on the mountaintop indicating that he has reached his goal. We must do the same.

Virgo, an earth sign, is the sixth sign of the zodiac. It is practical, materialistic, and reliable. It rejects the imperfect, is idealistic, and discriminating.

IX

THE HERMIT.

THE HERMIT UPRIGHT IN A SPREAD

Having the wisdom through experience and now able to function in a more positive way. Seeking a teacher or guide. Desire to learn meditation for spiritual guidance. New lessons in work or relationships. Getting advice from one you trust and respect. Setting up new goals for inner advancement. Tolerance. Completing a project. Plans for a trip. Meetings with an older male (parent).

THE HERMIT REVERSED IN A SPREAD

Person lacks wisdom or insight. Selfish and intolerant. Critical and judgmental views. Not open to new information. Sexual inhibitions. Closed minded and prejudiced. Feeling misunderstood. Not seeking spiritual enlightenment. Fear and guilt. Delayed plans and stagnation. Person focused on physical and material needs.

NINE OF WANDS

NINE OF WANDS UPRIGHT IN A SPREAD

Using wisdom in work and social activities. Knowing how to protect your interests in business and relationships. Using fair tactics in all dealings. Achievement through intelligence. Overcoming competition.

NINE OF WANDS REVERSED IN A SPREAD

Lacking wisdom or experience in work or society. Unwise plans cause despair. Open to abuse from outside sources, in business or relationships. Lack of confidence in creative abilities. Success difficult. Not a stable personality.

thoughts & feelings 1st read

NINE OF CUPS

NINE OF CUPS UPRIGHT IN A SPREAD

The Wish card! If the card is up—you get your wish. Wisdom in love and emotions. Putting love on a higher plane. Self-confidence in emotional experiences. Sexual fulfillment. Intuition good at this time. Healing ability through love.

NINE OF CUPS REVERSED IN A SPREAD

Lack of wisdom through experiences in love. Emotional drain due to loss, separation, or other negative events. Sexual overdrive. Indulgences and excesses. Inexperience. Thrill seeker. Conceit. Unenlightened.

NINE OF PENTACLES

NINE OF PENTACLES UPRIGHT IN A SPREAD
Wisdom through experience with money. Financial independence resulting from wise investments. Freedom from cares. Healthy existence. Use of creative talents produces economic well-being. Inheritance potential. Making right choices with money.

NINE OF PENTACLES REVERSED IN A SPREAD
Lack of wisdom in money matters, Loss through friends or wrong investments. Dependency needs create depression. Insecurity. Must learn to use discipline in financial matters. Health problems. spendthrift.

outside influences — 1st read

NINE OF SWORDS

NINE OF SWORDS UPRIGHT IN A SPREAD

Experiences in problems and troubles bring wisdom. Despair. A crisis period. Despondency. Quarrels. Suffering from effects of a loss, separation or misunderstanding. Mental anguish. Illness. Must redirect the energy. Let go of negative experiences and seek happiness now.

NINE OF SWORDS REVERSED IN A SPREAD

Experiences have not brought wisdom or understanding. Heading for a crisis period. Problems and troubles may become insurmountable—but the lessons must be learned. Time to make changes now, Low self-esteem. Use intuition to solve problems. Have faith in yourself.

WHEEL ᴏғ FORTUNE.

X WHEEL OF FORTUNE

Key Words: Changes, Cycles   *Minor Arcana:* Tens

Ruled by: Jupiter   *Element:* Fire

Positive Attributes: Success, Changes, Travel, New activity, Timing, Happiness, Meditation, Evolution

Negative Attributes: Stagnation, Physical focus, Fear of change, Unhappiness, Limited understanding, Unsuccessful, Gambling, Guilt

The Wheel of Fortune symbolizes major changes in life. The four elements are depicted in the four corners of the card and also in the second circle. The four symbols represent the elements in their natural state—Mercury, Salt, Sulfur, and Ether. The figures in the corners are shown in early stages of growth. The sphinx sits calmly above watching the wheel of karma slowly turning. The letters around the wheel spell "Rota"—the Royal Road and also Tarot. The figure ascending, Hermanubus, has the body of man and the head of a jackal. Jackals are known for their superb eyesight. The serpent is sexual energy, wisdom and temptation. The four figures represent the fixed signs of the zodiac—Taurus, Leo, Scorpio and Aquarius.

Jupiter (planet) rules Sagittarius, ninth sign of the zodiac. A fire planet (energy, action), Jupiter rules religion, law, philosophy, higher learning, and the search for truth.

WHEEL of FORTUNE.

WHEEL OF FORTUNE
UPRIGHT IN A SPREAD

Time now to make changes, take a chance on a new venture or travel. Gamble for fun or profit. Let go of old ties in business or relationships that are a burden. New experiences are available in areas of your life. Get married or engaged. Seek happiness during this peak period. Make plans for that trip you want. The time is ripe for success. Be positive and healthy.

WHEEL OF FORTUNE
REVERSED IN A SPREAD

No changes at this time. Do not gamble or take undue risks. Use honest tactics in all dealings. Success is elusive now. This is not the time to begin new ventures or serious relationships. Take care of diet and health needs. Travel plans may not materialize. Sexual desires are in focus.

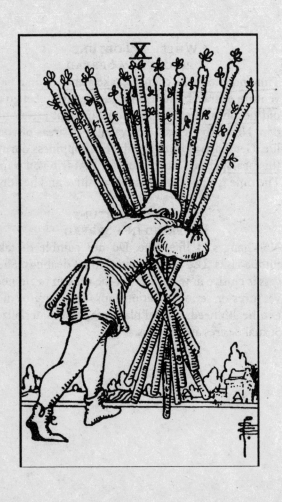

TEN OF WANDS

TEN OF WANDS UPRIGHT IN A SPREAD

Major changes at work or in social activities. Laying down burdens. New business methods or a new job opportunity. Social life becomes more active. Travel for business or pleasure. A good change.

TEN OF WANDS REVERSED IN A SPREAD

No changes in the work. Stagnant conditions bring despair. Obstacles to new plans are frustrating. Social life at low ebb. Heavy burdens cannot be released at this time. Feeling trapped at work. Little confidence in self. Lacking faith.

TEN OF CUPS

TEN OF CUPS UPRIGHT IN A SPREAD
Changes in love and emotions. New cycle in family relations. Love on a higher plane. A move or short trip. New love relationship. Happiness and harmony. Emotional well-being. Joy in the home and in family matters. Potential for good fortune.

TEN OF CUPS REVERSED IN A SPREAD
An emotional drain through family affairs. Over-indulgence results in ill health. Loss, separation, or depression. Feeling betrayed. Problems with children. Unhappy love relationship. Focus is on sexual needs. Tears. Broken promises.

TEN OF PENTACLES

TEN OF PENTACLES UPRIGHT IN A SPREAD

Major changes in finances. Acquisition of home or business. Inheritance. Unexpected trips. Financial security through others. Success in money matters. A marriage for money and security. Materialistic. Good health. Better times ahead.

TEN OF PENTACLES REVERSED IN A SPREAD

No changes in the financial picture. Family misfortune with money. Older people or relatives may be a burden monetarily. Loss of inheritance. Gambling. Spendthrift. Pay attention to health needs.

TEN OF SWORDS

TEN OF SWORDS UPRIGHT IN A SPREAD

Big changes in problems and troubles. Burdens will be removed. Back problems eased. Querent feels pinned down and unable to move. Negative cycle now ending. Need to exercise mentally, meditate, and work with the chakras, energy centers. Check unfavorable desires.

TEN OF SWORDS REVERSED IN A SPREAD

No changes in problems and troubles, but no new ones. Need to have the courage to rise again. Situation not as black as it appears. Physical desires are too important. Stagnation causes misery. Excessive burdens result in back problems. Mental focus unclear.

JUSTICE .

XI JUSTICE

Key Words: Justice, Equilibrium

Ruled by: Libra   *Element:* Air

Positive Attributes: Balance, Law, Harmony, Karma, Fairness, Moderation, Equality

Negative Attributes: Imbalance, Disharmony, Dishonesty, Criminality, Indecision, Paranoia, Rebellion

The Justice card refers to the equilibrium of opposing forces such as good and evil, light and dark, male and female, etc. Justice indicates legal matters, mercy, truth, harmony, and friendship. Karmic action and reaction. The scales of justice weigh each of us and the sword of truth ever hangs over our heads. The crown shows authority. In this card we see that justice is not blind. The cape is green, color of Venus (love and growth). The two pillars refer to the pairs of opposites in balance. Purple is the color of royalty. In days gone by the kings and queens handed out justice. The two-edged sword shows discrimination and right use of mental powers.

Libra, an air (mental) sign, is the seventh sign of the zodiac. It is the sign of partnerships, relationships, contracts, marriage, balance, law, open enemies, and decision making.

XI

JUSTICE .

JUSTICE UPRIGHT IN A SPREAD

Seeking justice in business or personal affairs. Legal matters need to be resolved fairly. Unfair treatment causes resentment and frustration. Moderation brings happiness. Potential for marriage. A successful legal battle and settlement. An authority figure on your side. Old karma removed by kindness and caring attitudes. Balance.

JUSTICE REVERSED IN A SPREAD

Legal complications due to anger and hostility. Uncompromising attitudes surround you. Prejudiced views. Overconfidence can lead to failure. Lack of balance and little happiness at this time. Mental depression as a result of unfair practices. Intemperate. Potential health problems.

THE HANGED MAN.

XII THE HANGED MAN

Key Words: Sacrifice, Reversal

Ruled by: Neptune   *Element:* Water

Positive Attributes: Trials, Duty, Faith, Contemplation, Surrender, Intuition, Discipline, Suspended mind

Negative Attributes: Foolish actions, Fantasy, Indecision, Escapism, Lack of faith, Fear and guilt, Undisciplined, Unstable

The Hanged Man is suspended from a living Tree of Life. He is bound by duty and necessity. He must surrender to a higher source within. Growth potential is shown by the green leaves on the Tree and green is Venus, planet of love. By means of meditation the Hanged Man overcomes temptation and becomes enlightened. The aura surrounding his head is yellow, color of Mercury—the mind. His crossed legs reveal the hidden language of limitation and expansion available to all of humanity. The Hanged Man is bound to the Tree by his ankle which is ruled by Aquarius, sign of the mind. We must reverse our opinions about the world around us.

Neptune rules Pisces, twelfth sign of the zodiac. Planet symbolizes beauty, the sea, dreams, prophecy, music, and psychic ability. It can also show fantasy and illusion.

THE HANGED MAN.

THE HANGED MAN UPRIGHT IN A SPREAD

Sacrificed to the will and desires of others. Time to meditate on inner sources and have faith. In bondage to personal views which may not be correct. Some trial or duty to family or friends. Illusory ideas without substance. Must learn to keep our feet on the ground and stay in balance. Positive growth through spiritual studies. Be creative and stay healthy.

THE HANGED MAN REVERSED IN A SPREAD

Procrastination. Easily fooled by others. Irresponsible actions. Little or no trust in a higher power. Not open to new information of a spiritual nature. Gullible. Drugs or liquor used for escapism. Focus is on physical and material needs. Refusing to meditate. Selfishness.

DEATH.

XIII DEATH

Key Words: Transformation

Ruled by: Scorpio   *Element:* Water

Positive Attributes: Renewal, Endings, Destruction and rebirth, Action, Immortality, New ideas, Physical change, Regeneration

Negative Attributes: Decay, Frustration, Inaction, Ignorance, Mortality, Sexuality, Materiality, Resentment

The Death card symbolizes the transforming powers of life and death. Death is the perpetual movement of creation for more perfect expression. The banner contains the mystical white rose, sign of pure love. The rose with its five petals refers to the five senses, immortality and the heart (when it is white). The sun rising denotes resurrection. The stream of water, subconsciousness, flows from the High Priestess card. No one is immune to the Reaper (Saturn) regardless of age, wealth, or position. We must all accept change as a necessity of life. Saturn also represents the bony structure of the body. The white horse depicts the five senses purified. The priest is a sign of faith and a belief in a higher power.

Scorpio, eighth sign of the zodiac, is a water sign—feminine, intuitive, subconsciousness, and emotional. Scorpio is the sign of death, sex, regeneration, other people's money, intensity, and secretiveness.

DEATH.

DEATH UPRIGHT IN A SPREAD

The end of a situation and a change for the better. New ideas and future plans are healthy. An inheritance or money coming to you from some source. Use energy to gain enlightenment. Let go of old experiences that no longer have meaning. Make a commitment now. Release resentments and be open to love. Take care of health issues

DEATH REVERSED IN A SPREAD

Stagnation, frustration, and unhappiness. Relationships not working well. Jealousy, anger, and resentment can affect your health. Lost love. Sexual needs may create problems. Too materialistic. Fear of death. No interest in spiritual knowledge. Little faith. Make decisions and set new goals for the future.

TEMPERANCE.

XIV TEMPERANCE

Key Words: Moderation, Tests, Trials

Ruled by: Sagittarius   *Element:* Fire

Positive Attributes: Balanced actions, Adjustments, Self-control, Guidance, Purification, Patience, Aspiration

Negative Attributes: Disharmony, Lack of self-control, Dishonesty, Ignorance, Wanderlust, Intolerance, Immoderate

The Temperance card refers to moderation, balance and harmony. All experiences are guided by our Higher Self with love and compassion. The angel is Michael (spirit of fire and the sun). Temperance shows the ability to equalize and harmonize self-consciousness with subconsciousness. Be aware that we do nothing of ourselves and we must learn to rely on our inner teacher and guide. The letters on the robe worn by Michael (at the neck) are "Yod-Heh-Vav-Heh" the name JEHOVAH. The Sun is rising in the north, place of greatest darkness. The pool is a feminine symbol. The triangle refers to the element of fire; the square is a symbol of earth and balance.

Sagittarius, ninth sign of the zodiac is a fire sign—energy, activity, and aspirations. Sagittarius is the sign of travel, outdoor sports, exercise, religion, philosophy, and law.

TEMPERANCE.

TEMPERANCE UPRIGHT IN A SPREAD

Positive use of energy, self-control, and harmony. Trusting the inner self for guidance. Meditation increases wisdom. Making plans to travel. Balancing emotions. Patience during difficult experiences. Tempering ego needs. Potential for learning a new skill or a short course pertaining to a hobby.

TEMPERANCE REVERSED IN A SPREAD

Self-indulgent, restless, and lacking patience at this time. Uncontrolled passions or desires can lead to trouble and defeat. A push for freedom can bring waste, loss, or misfortune. Negative use of sexual energy. Egotism. An emotional drain and unhappiness. Ignorance of higher laws or an inner source. Little faith.

THE DEVIL.

XV THE DEVIL

Key Words: Materialism, Deception

Ruled by: Capricorn *Element:* Earth

Positive Attributes: Health issues, Lifting the veil, Need to diet, Changed views, Desire for release, Responsibility, Search for truth

Negative Attributes: Greed, Depression, Bondage, Desires, Reverse thinking, Temptation, Irresponsibility, Wasted energy, Superficiality

The Devil is a mythical creature with no substance. He has been manifested by mankind through ignorance and a lack of personal responsibility. The Devil refers to the use of lower instincts to acquire physical and material possessions. We must endeavor to balance our subconscious and self-conscious minds. By trusting our Higher Self to lead and guide us we are granted our abundance now. We then free ourselves and are no longer prisoners of our lower instincts. The reverse pentagram is man turned upside down and a symbol of black magic. Through meditation, quieting our mind, we can see the truth about the Devil. The sign on the upraised hand of the Devil is Saturn—referring to limitation, organization, and testing. Saturn is the planet that rules Capricorn.

Capricorn, tenth sign of the zodiac, is an earth sign—material, physical. It is the sign of career, executive abilities, social standing, drive, and desire to get to the top.

THE DEVIL .

THE DEVIL UPRIGHT IN A SPREAD

Being bound to the world by physical and material greed. Desire for social success and acceptance at any cost. Seeing illusions rather than facing truth. Little sense of humor. Distorted picture of life and its meaning. Creative energy wasted in pleasure and overindulgences.

THE DEVIL REVERSED IN A SPREAD

Less selfishness or greed for material possessions or social standing. Refusing to worship false gods. Desire to face reality—to lift the veil of illusion. Desire to accept responsibility. Change of diet creates better health. Using creative abilities in beneficial ways.

THE TOWER.

XVI THE TOWER

Key Word: Catastrophe

Ruled by: Mars   *Element:* Fire

Positive Attributes: Unexpected changes, Karmic actions, New insights, Release of old habits, Ambition, Inspiration, Illumination

Negative Attributes: Impulsiveness, Lack of self-control, Selfishness, Sexual focus, Anger, Strife, Ignorance, Inactivity

The Tower represents the body of man. False ideas and old habit patterns must be relinquished to avoid catastrophic events. The lightning flash striking the crown (head) indicates mental illumination, light, and new information which changes our lives. The peak is the same as in Key 9, The Hermit. The falling figures are male (self-conscious) and female (subconscious). These are old ideas being thrown out of the body making room for new insights. The three openings refer to the trinity and fire energy. The yods, 10 on the right side, point to Key 10, The Wheel of Fortune, and the 10 spheres of the Qabalistic Tree of Life. The 12 yods on the left point to Key 12, The Hanged Man and the 12 connecting paths of the Tree of Life. (See the 10 of Pentacles for the Tree of Life.)

Mars rules Aries and is co-ruler of Scorpio. Mars is a fire planet—energy, desire, war, and action. It rules athletes, warfare, independence, initiative, and leadership.

THE TOWER.

THE TOWER UPRIGHT IN A SPREAD

Overthrow of false ideas and old habit patterns. Potential catastrophe due to negative actions recently or from the past. Sudden events. Strife and discord regarding relationships, family members, or friends. Accepting changes releases fear and promotes better health conditions. New insights bring hope and faith. A need to curb speech and spend time alone.

THE TOWER REVERSED IN A SPREAD

Refusing to change old habit patterns. The focus is on sexuality, jealousy, and resentment. Fear, frustration, and danger from unseen sources. Limited understanding. Freedom is in jeopardy. Financial troubles. Wrong use of will. Materialistic views.

THE STAR.

XVII THE STAR

Key Words: Discovery, Aspiration

Ruled by: Aquarius   *Element:* Air

Positive Attributes: Meditation, Enlightenment, Inspiration, Optimism, Achievement, Goal setting, Creativity

Negative Attributes: Doubts, Pessimism, Unstable attitude, Loneliness, Little ambition, Imbalance, Inflexibility

The Star card refers to meditation and setting goals in life. "Hitching your wagon to a star" and winning! The seven small stars point to the seven chakras, seven astrological planets, and the seven alchemical metals. The chakras are energy sources located along the spine. The stars are eight-pointed (Key 8, Strength). The bird is an ibis and it belongs to Hermes, Mercury (messenger of the gods). The figure has the right foot in water, blending subconsciousness with self-consciousness, The figure is nude, showing openness, honesty, and nothing to hide. The vases represent physical manifestation.

Aquarius, the eleventh sign of the zodiac, is an Air sign—mental. It is the sign of freedom, change, travel, statesmanship, humanitarianism, the public, and invention and includes friends, hopes, and wishes.

THE STAR.

THE STAR UPRIGHT IN A SPREAD

Faith and trust in life. Setting new goals for the future. New opportunities in career or relationships. Friendship is important. Don't waste time or energy in trivial pursuits. A desire to know truth. Be optimistic and have the courage to follow new pathways. Maintain balance in all endeavors.

THE STAR REVERSED IN A SPREAD

Pessimistic about career moves, relationships, and life in general. No new goals for the future adds to feelings of boredom. End of friendship or marriage brings sadness. Health problems and mental discontent. Scattered energy. Stubbornness. Fear of trying new ways. Little ambition or drive. Low self-esteem.

THE MOON.

XVIII THE MOON

Key Words: Attainment

Ruled by: Pisces   *Element:* Water

Positive Attributes: Imagination, Dreams, The unknown, Reflection, Illusion, Emotions, Spirituality

Negative Attributes: Fantasy, Deception, Impatience, Intolerance, Treachery, Restlessness, Unwise desires

The Moon card is a symbol of time and reflected light. The full Moon can create mental unrest, depression and melancholy. From the subconsciousness (pool) come our fears, desires and passions. We must understand this and guide ourselves with love and compassion. The Moon card refers to emotions, intuition, psychic ability and cycles. The New Moon is the time to begin new projects in a personal sense or in the public arena. The wolf is a symbol of untamed animalistic tendencies within each person. The dog has been domesticated and is friendly. The crayfish crawling out of subconsciousness indicates the early stages of thought. The towers in the distance are not the end of the path, but a higher stage of attainment as we proceed. They have the same meaning as the pillars we have seen in other cards.

Pisces, twelfth sign of the zodiac, is a water sign—emotional, female, and intuitive. Pisces is the sign of creativity, psychic ability, illusions, affections, martyrdom, and sympathy.

THE MOON .

THE MOON UPRIGHT IN A SPREAD

Deception and illusion, refusing to face the truth. Problems from secret enemies. Person must learn to control negative thinking. Fears and doubts about life and the future. Not using psychic ability or intuition to overcome difficulties. Swayed by emotions. Feeling victimized by others. Indecisiveness. Moody.

THE MOON REVERSED IN A SPREAD

Depression due to delayed plans. Emotions sublimated through fear and doubt. Health can be affected adversely. Feeling betrayed by someone close. Be careful of expectations. Uncontrolled desires may be harmful. Keep your feet on the ground and be sensible. Use artistic talents to best advantage. Trust yourself.

THE SUN .

XIX THE SUN

Key Words: Renewal

Ruled by: Leo   *Element:* Fire

Positive Attributes: Energy, Vitality, Confidence, Truth, Achievement, Talent, Success, Regeneration

Negative Attributes: Wasted talents, Unsound judgment, Arrogance, Less energy, Egotism, Expectations, Little self-esteem

The Sun is life, energy, vitality, ego and the desire to attain. The Sun card signifies liberation and new beginnings. The Sun is the source of our power. It is called our day star. The child is nude, which shows honesty, innocence, and openness. The sunflowers are life and the seeds are new ideas. The wall indicates limits in the physical world, although there are none in the spiritual world. The card also refers to the study of science and mathematics. The straight lines coming down from the sun are masculine; the wavy lines are feminine. The red banner shows energy and action. The horse refers to the five senses and also energy.

Leo, fifth sign of the zodiac, is a fire sign—activity, power, and drive. Leo is the sign of the ego, desire for praise, attention, applause, recognition, creativity, friendliness, and generosity.

THE SUN .

THE SUN UPRIGHT IN A SPREAD

Seeking truth and happiness. New work in science or mathematics. Having confidence in our abilities to bring success into our life. Open to new thought. Courage to carry out plans for the future. Material gain. Approval from others. Planning a trip for work or pleasure. Good health and vitality.

THE SUN REVERSED IN A SPREAD

Lack of courage or confidence is defeating. Low self-esteem. Sexual needs are the main issue. Low energy levels can lead to serious health problems. Dishonesty creates discord and loss of trust from others. Great expectations of other people will cause disappointments. Refusing to accept limits regardless of cost. Egotistical. Ostentatious.

JUDGEMENT.

XX JUDGMENT

Key Words: Awareness

Ruled by: Pluto   *Element:* Water

Positive Attributes: Faith, Inner listening, Immortality, Higher Mind, Awakening to truth, Right judgment, Understanding

Negative Attributes: Lacking faith, Materialism, Confusion, Being unaware, Fear and guilt, Physical focus, Mortality

The Judgment card refers to conscience, the Higher Self within and immortality. The angel is Gabriel calling us to become aware of the Source within. The seven tones emitted from the trumpet signify the seven chakras, the seven planets, the seven candlesticks and the seven seals. The Judgment card shows us turning away from traditional teachings to new knowledge of immortality. The banner (white, purity) with the red cross refers to the four elements, fire, air, water and earth, all in balance. The child represents the new birth in consciousness. The coffins are symbols for the physical body in which the soul is entombed.

Pluto rules Scorpio, a water sign and the eighth sign of the zodiac. Pluto is the planet of generation, regeneration, destruction, the underworld, masses, phobias, crime, groups, and transformation.

JUDGEMENT.

Judgement Upright in a Spread

Faith in a Higher Power within. New knowledge brings joy and happiness. Refusing to accept traditional views. Change of residence, new position or career. Spiritual attunement and trusting the self. Health improvement. New understanding brings added confidence. Study of New Age material answers perplexing questions.

Judgement Reversed in a Spread

Materialistic approach to life. Blind faith and mistaken judgments. Fear of New Age material. Apprehensive about changes. Tunnel vision. Belief in mortality. Loss or separation from family and or friends. Health issues. A need to face the truth. Traditional thinking.

THE WORLD.

XXI THE WORLD

Key Words: Cosmic Consciousness

Ruled by: Saturn   *Element:* Earth

Positive Attributes: Completion, Victory, Knowledge, Salvation, Success, Reward, Insight, Fulfillment

Negative Attributes: Anxiety, Limitation, Materialistic, Mistrust, Unwise actions, Closed mind, Stubborn

The World card shows balance and support by unseen forces. The central figure is androgynous indicating all of humanity. This is the final card of the Major Arcana and represents completion, fulfillment and total understanding. The figure in each of the four corners has been seen previously in Key 10, the Wheel of Fortune. These four figures have changed dramatically during their experiences in life. The figures are: lower left—Taurus, earth; lower right—Leo, fire; upper left—Aquarius, air; upper right—Scorpio, water. The elliptical shape of the wreath alludes to superconsciousness. The ribbons on the top and bottom are shaped like figure eights, meaning eternity and strength. The wreath also indicates success and victory in life.

Saturn rules Capricorn, tenth sign of the zodiac. It is the planet of discipline, organization, limitation, awareness, and time.

THE WORLD.

THE WORLD UPRIGHT IN A SPREAD

Success in all endeavors and the attainment of all goals. Long journey proves beneficial. New opportunities offered. A new job, career change, or move. Feeling supported by inner resources. Inheritance or some material gain. Ability to maintain balance in any crisis. Victory! Faith and trust in a Higher Source.

THE WORLD REVERSED IN A SPREAD

No success or material gain. Plans delayed or defeated. Lacking vision or truth. Feeling unsupported and vulnerable to outside influences. Frustrating limitations. Fear of change or the unknown. Unbalanced emotions. Illusion and deception. Little mental growth. Physical and sexual desires are in demand.

COURT CARDS

The final sixteen cards (Court Cards) are represented by: Kings, Queens, Pages, and Knights.

These cards represent influences in the environment such as: friends, family members, lovers, and people in the marketplace. They can refer to ideas in the mind of the Querent.

The Court Cards have individual astrological signs and physical characteristics, so they are easily identifiable. When they are upright they indicate positive traits of that person or idea. When reversed, they show: a negative influence, a female in the case of a reversed King, or a male in the case of a reversed Queen.

If a Court Card is the final card in a reading:

- The event will occur at the time of the astrological sign of that card

- The Querent (questioner) will receive information from another person

- The Querent is waiting for someone else to make the decisions regarding the question

KINGS

Age 35 or older. Kings signify a father figure, authority, wisdom, and experience.

QUEENS

Age 35 or older. Queens signify a mother image, authority figure, maturity, nurturing, and understanding.

KNIGHTS

Age 25 to 35 (40). Knights are also messengers. They can be male or female. The message is positive when right side up, negative when reversed.

PAGES

Age 1 to 21 (25). Pages represent children in various stages of growth and experience. They can indicate messengers, schoolchildren, young adults, and assorted problems.

SOME SAMPLES USING COURT CARDS

If a King is next to a Page it might suggest:

- A man and his son

- A man acting like a child

- A man involved with a younger person, same or different sex

If a King and Queen are side by side:

- Husband and wife

- Parents of Querent, other relatives, or older people in the environment

If a King, Queen, and Page are together:

- A family unit (Querent's)

- Problems between parents and child

- Child comes between parents if the Page card is shown between the King and Queen

- Check the direction the Court Cards are facing; if away, the person is not interested in the situation

If two Queens are side by side:

- Friends, lovers, or relatives

If Queen and Page are side by side:

- Mother and son or daughter
- A woman involved with a younger lover
- Immature older woman

If several Kings are in the spread:

- Problems with authority figures or police

If several Queens are in the spread:

- Social gathering or special meetings

If several Pages are in the spread:

- Youngsters involved with Querent, party time, or friends

If several Knights are in the spread:

- Messages regarding business or pleasure; people of that age in the environment

Our society has become very diverse. Males and females now work in the same positions, making differentiation difficult. A woman may be seen through a male card due to her position and authority, whereas a man might be identified through a female card. This occurs frequently with the Court Cards.

KING of WANDS

KING OF WANDS

Ruled by: Aries (March 21 to April 20)

Time: Weeks

PHYSICAL CHARACTERISTICS

Reddish complexion, light to medium hair color, body leans forward, long or blunt nose, and forehead slopes slightly.

KING OF WANDS UPRIGHT IN A SPREAD

This King is independent, influential, and an authority in business. He is ambitious, has executive talents and leadership qualities. He is a good friend and loyal. The King of Wands enjoys starting new enterprises but does not usually stay for the finish. He is socially active and likes to entertain his family and friends. Potential for inheritance.

KING OF WANDS REVERSED IN A SPREAD

This King is childish, dependent, and shows antisocial behavior. He can be selfish, domineering, and a petty tyrant. He has relationship problems due to an overbearing, unyielding, and intolerant attitude. Head injuries happen frequently to this Aries type. This can be an Aries female when reversed—positive or negative.

KING of CUPS.

KING OF CUPS

Ruled by: Cancer (June 22 to July 23)

Time: Days

PHYSICAL CHARACTERISTICS
Large head and body, wide chest area, full lips, large eyes and small ears, broad hips.

KING OF CUPS UPRIGHT IN A SPREAD
This King is emotional, loving, caring, and nurturing. He is a good family man when married. His interests include real estate, home products, interior design, food, the arts, and science. The King of Cups needs to feel safe and secure in whatever profession he follows. He is a water sign and could be in the Navy as a career.

KING OF CUPS REVERSED IN A SPREAD
This King is cold, uncaring, and does not nurture others. He can be untrustworthy in love or business. His emotions are unstable and he can be ruthless and calculating. This King reversed shows fear and anxiety through a lack of security. This can be a Cancer female reversed—positive or negative.

KING of PENTACLES.

KING OF PENTACLES

Ruled by: Taurus (April 21 to May 21)

Time: Year

PHYSICAL CHARACTERISTICS
Medium to dark skin, thick body, broad shoulders, small ears, and large mouth. Short neck and dimples.

KING OF PENTACLES UPRIGHT IN A SPREAD
This King is a good financial advisor, practical, and reliable. He is a solid citizen, slow to anger but stubborn (bull-headed). Experienced in business, banking, and salesmanship. The King is a successful entrepreneur, helpful to friends, and family.

KING OF PENTACLES REVERSED IN A SPREAD
This Taurus King is selfish, lazy, a speculator and impractical with money. He loves luxury, is sensual, and desires pleasure. There is a tendency toward dishonesty and to use shady business practices. Potential for health problems. This can be a Taurus female when reversed—positive or negative.

KING of SWORDS.

KING OF SWORDS

Ruled by: Gemini (May 22 to June 21)

Time: Months

PHYSICAL CHARACTERISTICS

Long torso, broad shoulders, straight forehead, long straight nose. Long arms, hands, and fingers, pointed chin, and wide mouth.

KING OF SWORDS UPRIGHT IN A SPREAD

This King is a professional man, a lawyer or in the military. This card can also indicate the need for a lawyer. He has mental dexterity, is a good counselor, and has lots of nervous energy. The King is discriminating and has many friends. Little sentimentality.

KING OF SWORDS REVERSED IN A SPREAD

This King is fickle and superficial. He dissipates his energy. He is unkind with words, a gossip, and can be mentally unstable. He rebels against authority. Potential loss through a lawsuit. This King can be dishonest in business or with others. This can be a Gemini female when reversed—positive or negative.

QUEEN of WANDS.

QUEEN OF WANDS

Ruled by: Leo(July 24 to August 23)

Time: Weeks

PHYSICAL CHARACTERISTICS

Tall stature, large head, strong back, heavy nose, and regal bearing. She walks like a lion, taking long slow steps.

QUEEN OF WANDS UPRIGHT IN A SPREAD

This Queen desires success in work and social activities. She is a social lioness and a positive advisor. She is an authority figure, ambitious, and ego-driven to shine in all her endeavors. This Queen needs admiration and attention. She is a loyal friend and fun to be with. Her expectations are high at work and in social settings.

QUEEN OF WANDS REVERSED IN A SPREAD

The Queen of Wands reversed is domineering, demanding, and controlling at work or in social situations. She is unloving, peevish, and no fun to be with. Her ego needs drive her to ruthless actions and gossip. This Queen's business practices are not always honest. She is motivated by anger, resentment, and jealousy. This can be a Leo man when reversed—positive or negative.

QUEEN of CUPS.

QUEEN OF CUPS

Ruled by: Scorpio (October 24 to November 22)

Time: Days

PHYSICAL CHARACTERISTICS

Usually dark, prominent eyes, heavy eyebrows, large ears, high cheekbones, short to medium height. Tami ?

QUEEN OF CUPS UPRIGHT IN A SPREAD

This Queen is involved with love and emotions. She is a good wife and mother, very protective of her family. She is a sexual woman and loving. This Queen is powerful, intuitive, and intense. She is a good friend or an implacable enemy. She desires control in her environment. This Scorpio Queen is secretive and possessive.

QUEEN OF CUPS REVERSED IN A SPREAD

The Queen of Cups reversed is dishonest in love. Her emotions are being drained due to a loss, separation, or other unhappy events. The Queen has a bad temper, is involved in intrigue, and is the jealous type. She is resentful and harbors grudges. An unfaithful friend. This can be a Scorpio man when reversed—positive or negative.

QUEEN of PENTACLES

QUEEN OF PENTACLES

Ruled by: Virgo (August 24 to September 23)

Time: Year

PHYSICAL CHARACTERISTICS

Sturdy body, small-boned, high forehead, large ears, thin lips, and a sharp nose. Hair is light or medium brown.

QUEEN OF PENTACLES UPRIGHT IN A SPREAD

The Queen is involved with making money and also health matters. She is an idealist and a perfectionist. She has critical views. This Queen shows harvest time after much labor. This card can indicate a potential for pregnancy. Gifts from family or friends. Sexual focus.

QUEEN OF PENTACLES REVERSED IN A SPREAD

This Queen is a spendthrift and lazy. She is a superficial friend, lacks self-confidence, and is judgmental. The Queen of Pentacles reversed is discontented and feels imperfect. She can be cold or over-sexed. There could be a health problem. Lack of money. This can be a Virgo man—positive and negative.

QUEEN of SWORDS.

QUEEN OF SWORDS

Ruled by: Libra (September 24 to October 23)

Time: Months

PHYSICAL CHARACTERISTICS

Tall, usually lean body, long hands, fingers, and neck. A low forehead, full lips, beautiful skin and face, plus a shapely nose.

QUEEN OF SWORDS UPRIGHT IN A SPREAD

This Queen is associated with problems and troubles. She is often a divorced woman, a widow, or single. The Queen is strong-willed, sharp-tongued, and temperamental. She needs a relationship because Libra is the sign of marriage. She has difficulties making decisions. Legal matters may be pending and need attention.

QUEEN OF SWORDS REVERSED IN A SPREAD

This Queen has problems and troubles but may not wish to confront them. She fears divorce or separation with any of her relationships. Her sexual needs are an important issue in her life. The Queen is ambitious but not always open or honest with others. Mental anxieties. This can be a Libra man when reversed—positive or negative.

KNIGHT of WANDS.

KNIGHT OF WANDS

Ruled by: Leo (July 24 to August 23)

Time: Weeks

KNIGHT OF WANDS UPRIGHT IN A SPREAD
This messenger brings information concerning work and social activities. There is good news relating to work, planning for a trip, or a change of residence. Good tidings regarding relationships, news of a marriage, and or other happy events. The Knight likes action.

KNIGHT OF WANDS REVERSED IN A SPREAD
This messenger brings negative news regarding work and social activities. The news causes delays and frustration in the job and also affects a social event. The Knight can be upset and angry due to his expectations being denied. Canceled trip. Egotistical actions.

KNIGHT of CUPS.

KNIGHT OF CUPS

Ruled by: Scorpio (October 24 to November 22)

Time: Days

KNIGHT OF CUPS UPRIGHT IN A SPREAD

Messages are positive regarding love and emotions.
The Knight brings new information concerning a
birth, invitation to a party or wedding. His messages
are intense and they refer to a close relationship or
some family matter. The Knight is a loving, sensual,
and sexual person, a good companion who can be
generous. New travel plans with a friend or lover.

KNIGHT OF CUPS REVERSED IN A SPREAD

These messages concerning love and emotions do
not arrive, or if they do, they bring unhappy news.
This Knight reversed shows an emotional drain
involving relationships, friendships, or family. A
potential loss or separation from a loved one. This
Knight is a procrastinator and can be dishonest.

KNIGHT of PENTACLES.

KNIGHT OF PENTACLES

Ruled by: Taurus (April 21 to May 21)

Time: Year

KNIGHT OF PENTACLES UPRIGHT IN A SPREAD

This Knight brings communications involving money. Good news about an inheritance, real estate, or other valuables. This Knight has lots of energy and good health. He also has many desires, is sensual/sexual, and enjoys material possessions. Money repaid by a friend. Salary increase at work.

KNIGHT OF PENTACLES REVERSED IN A SPREAD

Messages not received or they bring unhappy news. The messages show a lack of finances which causes delays or failure to existing plans. Loss of valuables or other assets at this time. This Knight can be lazy, oversexed, and passionate but refuses to resolve money problems. Depression and inertia.

KNIGHT of SWORDS.

KNIGHT OF SWORDS

Ruled by: Aquarius (January 21 to February 19)

Time: Months

KNIGHT OF SWORDS UPRIGHT IN A SPREAD

This messenger brings news of problems and troubles. These messages may relate to you personally or someone close to you (family or friend). The messages are filled with conflicts, anger, and feelings of frustration. The Knight of Swords shows aggressive behavior which is mentally, usually not physically, violent. This Knight could be a person in one of the services—Army, Navy, Marines.

KNIGHT OF SWORDS REVERSED IN A SPREAD

Messages sent with this Knight may or may not be received. The news concerns problems and troubles. Person sending the information is indifferent and refuses to give any consideration to the problems or troubles now. This Knight is closed mentally and unreliable. Health needs attention. Hopes and desires not satisfied.

PAGE of WANDS.

PAGE OF WANDS

Ruled by: Sagittarius (November 23 to December 21)

Time: Weeks

PHYSICAL CHARACTERISTICS
Often tall and slender, long legs, ears prominent, long nose, skin usually medium to dark.

PAGE OF WANDS UPRIGHT IN A SPREAD
This page is eager to experience work and social activities. He or she desires freedom, is headstrong, and independent. The Page has great expectations and has luck on his side. International travel, foreign foods, meeting foreign people, and the study of philosophy are many of this Page's needs. Action is the aim and goal of the Page. Good news about work or social experiences.

PAGE OF WANDS REVERSED IN A SPREAD
The reversed Page can be lazy and immoral, refusing to work or be involved in society. He or she can be fickle, faithless, cruel, and extravagant. This Page is known to gossip or betray confidences. The Page may be a "stay at home," fear outside influences, or foreigners. Many obstacles. Unwelcome news.

PAGE of CUPS.

PAGE OF CUPS

Ruled by: Pisces (February 20 to March 20)

Time: Days

PHYSICAL CHARACTERISTICS

Willowy body, large feet, expressive hands, protruding eyes, and pale skin. Hair color—light to medium.

PAGE OF CUPS UPRIGHT IN A SPREAD

The Page of Cups refers to love and emotions. He or she has psychic ability and is very creative. This page can also be a healer. The Page brings good news concerning love relationships, parties, births, and marriages. This Page can be illusory, oversensitive, or a homosexual. Problems associated with liquor or drugs.

PAGE OF CUPS REVERSED IN A SPREAD

This Page reversed shows an emotional drain and many disappointments. He or she has great expectations which may not be fulfilled. Unhappy news concerning relationships and a fear of rejection. This Page may be experiencing emotional abuse and a lack of love. The Page is not using creative talents or his or her psychic ability at this time.

PAGE of PENTACLES.

PAGE OF PENTACLES

Ruled by: Capricorn (December 22 to January 20)

Time: Year

PHYSICAL CHARACTERISTICS

Dark skin and hair. Big-boned, large head, and sharp nose. Usually stocky and not always tall. Long-lived.

PAGE OF PENTACLES UPRIGHT IN A SPREAD

This Page has the desire for money. He or she is interested in schooling, a career, and reaching the top of their profession. This is the card of the student. The Page is materialistic, ambitious, and traditional. He or she can try to use others for gain or to help attain specific goals. Positive messages regarding money and health issues.

PAGE OF PENTACLES REVERSED IN A SPREAD

This Page is not interested in schooling, setting goals, or learning how to earn money. He or she prefers the easy life, is selfish, greedy, and lazy. The Page resents authority and is very demanding. The messages from this Page are not positive and concern money and health matters.

PAGE of SWORDS.

PAGE OF SWORDS

Ruled by: Aquarius (January 21 to February 19)

Time: Months

PHYSICAL CHARACTERISTICS

Medium to tall stature, erect carriage, large head, high forehead, round eyes, and broad shoulders.

PAGE OF SWORDS UPRIGHT IN A SPREAD

This Page deals with problems and troubles. He or she desires novel experiences, new knowledge, and many friendships The Page is extroverted, naive, and unconventional. He or she has many desires, hopes, and wishes. The Page is motivated by mental concerns about other people in trouble. New adventures can create strife.

PAGE OF SWORDS REVERSED IN A SPREAD

This Page has some problems and troubles and is not a free thinker. He or she is less stable mentally. Friendships are not as important to this Page. He or she is more introverted, anxious, and paranoid. Hopes and wishes are not being fulfilled. Not a humanitarian or interested in others.

TAROT SPREADS

There are many interesting spreads in use today. Tarot readers usually have the desire to create their own special spreads which work well for them. Many readers select a variety of spreads and rearrange them to suit their needs. An astrological student studying Tarot decided to enlarge the Horoscope spread. She added three cards each to the Aries, Cancer, Libra, and Capricorn Houses. In addition, she placed three more cards in the center of the wheel for information regarding the future. Another student worked with a pyramid spread in an unconventional manner. She read from the top down relating all the cards to the present, and she was very accurate.

The idea of using one particular spread can aid your subconscious mind to focus better. The intention is to become comfortable and relaxed during the reading, and the more familiar the spread the quicker the intuition begins to operate. Begin with a short spread (Celtic) to give you the confidence you need and then progress to a longer one.

The following pages contain spreads plus sample readings to help you define and interpret the cards when doing your own readings. If you want additional information, two books exclusively about spreads are *Classic Tarot Spreads* by Sandor Konraad and *How to Read the Tarot* by Doris Doane and K. Keyes.

CELTIC SPREAD

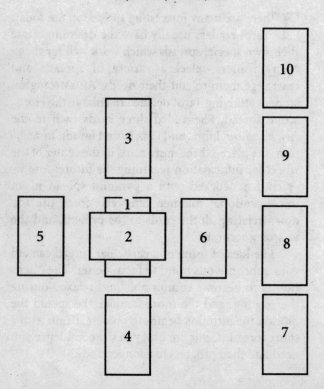

1. Concern

2. Obstacles

3. Objective

4. Thoughts/Feelings

5. Past

6. Immediate future

7. Attitude about the question

8. Outside influences

9. Hopes and fears

10. Final Outcome

CELTIC SPREAD SAMPLE READING

This is a reading for Fern, a Cancer sign. Her question concerned her work. She wanted to know if her job change was going to make her happy and what effect it would have on her finances.

1. Concern: 7 of Pentacles

Fern is thinking about money and her job. She must think of ways to increase her financial position. The path she takes will bring prosperity and victory. She is concerned due to the big shakeup and pay cut at work.

2. The Obstacles: Empress

Fern feels they don't appreciate her at work. She is a communicator, creative, and wants to enjoy her job. She is a supervisor with little or no power. (The Empress signifies authority.)

3. The Objective: Queen of Pentacles reversed

Perhaps Fern would rather not work. Her objective could be to find a job more suitable or work out of her home. She is discontented and unhappy with her boss for several reasons including his lack of support.

4. Thoughts/feelings: 6 of Pentacles

Fern is contemplating her choices, especially the financial angle. She may decide on other options rather than continuing with this company, where she has been employed for the last ten years.

5. Past Actions: Star

Fern had set high goals for herself in this job. She saw lots of opportunities for advancement and the financial rewards were substantial. She had been optimistic about her future with the company.

6. Immediate future: 4 of Swords

Fern is nervous and anxious about the coming move. This can adversely affect her health if she gets too depressed. Fern realizes she is not looking forward to the changes because her ride to work will be longer and her shift undesirable.

7. Attitude(Hers): Magician

Fern's attitude is that she will have to accept this new beginning until she can find another position. Perhaps a new relationship or marriage is possible for her. Something new and exciting or a new job would be a happy solution at this time.

8. Influences: Strength reversed
Fern feels she does not have enough strength to cope with the situation. Her family and friends are in no position to help her nor do they have any influence in this area. Many of her coworkers are in the same situation and are powerless to halt the changes for themselves.

9. Hopes/fears: King of Swords reversed
Several times in the past Fern had considered hiring a lawyer and suing for harassment, but never followed through. Due to the current state of affairs she feels she can sue her employer for discrimination and win. Fern is afraid that her coworkers will not join her in this legal suit.

10. Final Outcome: 3 of Cups reversed
Fern is experiencing an emotionally traumatic time in her life. Her personal relationship is satisfactory but she would like a commitment. Her work is unsettling. Both areas of her life need adjustments before she can be happy again.

There are six people or ideas in Fern's life which can create disruptions or interferences. Her thinking will not be as clear as it should be. Fern insists that money is not the prime issue, although for a Cancer, money is very important for security reasons reversed 3 of Cups tells Fern how unhappy she is emotionally, sexually, and mentally. The time for change is now.

Celtic Spread Sample Reading

The following is a reading for Morris, a Gemini. He is in partnership with an Aries female and a Cancer male. The question involves health issues and the continuation of their business.

1. The Concern: 3 of Pentacles

The concern for Morris is being creative and making money. He is a master craftsman. He enjoys his work and wants to be successful.

2. Obstacles: Sun

Morris feels he isn't getting the recognition or attention he desires for his efforts. He has confidence in his own abilities and may feel he would enjoy some new endeavor. The decline in the economy is affecting the business and this could be a contributing factor to his health problems. This card refers to the ego—this could also be part of the difficulty with Morris.

3. Objective: Ace of Cups

On an emotional level Morris might want to begin something new. He could make a move in either business or residence. Morris desires good health and well-being. By staying in the partnership he might feel that he could not accomplish his health goals.

4. Thoughts/feelings: 3 of Swords

Morris makes his own problems and troubles. There are three partners in the business and each one has their own ideas about how it should be run. This creates conflict between them. He may feel some animosity from the other two.

5. Past: 10 of Wands reversed

In the past Morris was not able to relieve himself of his burdens. He tried new plans but there were obstacles that he could not overcome. He began to feel trapped and lost some of his confidence.

6. Immediate future: Ace of Swords

There are new beginnings in problems and troubles. Morris has been told that he needs a heart operation and the sooner the better.

7. Attitudes (His): High Priestess

Morris is intelligent enough to know that he must take care of his health. He is intuitive and confident regarding the outcome of the operation. He has a good attitude which will aid his recovery. His wife is supportive and she is a professional career woman, High Priestess.

8. Outside influences: King of Cups reversed

The King of Cups represents one of the partners—a Cancer. Morris observed that this partner does not pay enough attention to business, is cold and indifferent. This is an intolerable situation and extremely irritating on a day to day basis.

9. Hopes/fears: 9 of Wands reversed

Morris hopes that his partners are equipped to handle the business while he is recuperating. His main fear is that they will not protect it or that they will make unwise decisions in his absence.

10. Final outcome: 9 of Swords

The outcome shows a crisis period for Morris. He may quarrel with his partners due to his own fears. He must redirect his energy into a more positive attitude and let go of his fears. Everything looks clearer in the daylight—solutions appear easier in the light.

Postscript

Morris had the operation and everything went great! During the second week after the event Morris went back to work for a few hours a day. Having a positive attitude did help Morris.

SEVENTEEN CARD SPREAD

1. Querent's concern
2. The conflict
3. Happiness or sadness
4. Conditions of health or security
5. Past actions affecting the first card
6. Immediate future
7. Character and ego traits of Querent
8. Outside influences affecting money and environment
9. Hopes and fears relating to the tenth card
10. Outcome
11. Past actions of family and friends
12. Illusions regarding question or secret enemies

13. Future plans
14. Past emotional concerns
15. 16. 17. Goals for the future

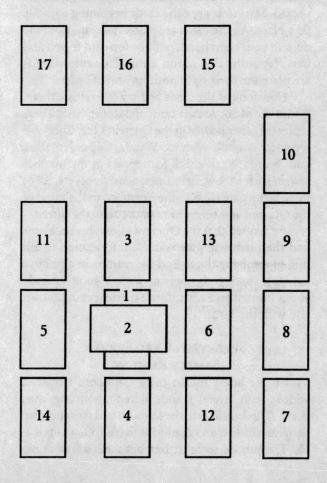

This spread is self-explanatory. After the Querent has shuffled the cards they are returned to you. Remember to tell the person to make a wish in the event the Wish card makes an appearance in the spread. Start to lay out the cards beginning with the first place. All the cards are placed face up. Hold the deck in your right hand, pull the top card to you and over, repeating this action until all seventeen cards are placed in their right position and in order.

Now look at the cards and try to evaluate them. Count the Major Arcana cards and Court cards. These represent other people in the Querent's life. Check for repeated symbols such as: Wands, Cups, Pentacles, and Swords. Next, check for repeats in the number system such as how many ones, twos, threes etc. All of these factors are clues to the questions in the mind of the Querent and help you to understand the spread.

Be assured that the Querent knows his problems and the cards will give you the information to aid him in resolving them. End the reading in a positive manner, leaving the person with a good attitude about himself and any future experiences of his own and with the Tarot.

SEVENTEEN CARD SPREAD
SAMPLE READING

This is a reading for an older Capricorn female, a widow, with several grandchildren whom she loves dearly. This lady lives in the Midwest and visits her son, daughter-in-law, and grandchildren as often as possible. The lady is a senior citizen but she is still working.

1. The concern: Page of Cups reversed

The Querent's concern is her Pisces granddaughter, age 22. The Querent is worried because the granddaughter has broken several bones in the past year, traveled around, and has not been willing to settle down. Recently the granddaughter returned to college to finish her studies, which has made this lady happy. The Querent feels emotionally drained.

2. The conflict: The Star

The Querent has high hopes and aspirations for her granddaughter and wishes her to succeed in life. The granddaughter has not felt the same way, but going back to school is a positive step for the girl.

3. Happiness or Sadness: 10 of Swords

This card indicates that the Querent's problems and troubles are changing. The burdens she has been carrying are beginning to lighten. Now the Querent must change her attitude and not be pessimistic. Happiness is contagious.

4. Health and Security: 2 of Wands

The Querent knows about work and social activities, she works four days a week. She has the world in her hands; her security is in her work and home. Conditions are healthy for the Querent and there is no need for her to worry.

5. Past actions affecting first card: Judgment

In the past the Querent was critical and judgmental in regard to her granddaughter's actions. The girl's parents are divorced. The Querent also realized that her granddaughter was very unhappy during her early formative years. The Querent was unable to change any of the conditions which made her unhappy.

6. Immediate future: 5 of Pentacles

This card implies money is worshiped as God. The Querent had financial problems on her mind. She needs to change her thinking about money and to believe in prosperity. Old thought habits (especially negative ones regarding finances) must be released.

7. Character and ego traits: King of Cups

The Querent identifies with this card (the Cancer type) loving, nurturing, sharing, and mothering. The benevolent mother taking care of her family (or father figure who sees himself in this role). This is the ideal.

8. Outside influences affecting environment and money: 4 of Swords

This card tells the Querent to rest and have faith. She must stop worrying and rebalance her health or suffer the consequences. She creates her own problems and troubles. The family is financially solvent with no immediate money problems.

9. Hopes and fears relating to tenth card: 2 of Swords

Querent knows about problems and troubles but refuses to see solutions. Meditation would help her see the truth. Perhaps she fears knowing too much.

10. Outcome: 4 of Wands

This card shows there is fruitfulness, balance, stability, and the possibility of a new home for the Querent. It can also indicate a potential marriage (the Querent, family member, or friend). By combining the ninth and tenth cards the Querent needs to evaluate her life and her family's to realize that there are many positive experiences she could be grateful for. Now is the time to enjoy her life without all the responsibilities of the past.

11. Past actions of family/friends:
7 of Swords reversed
In the past there were continual problems and troubles but not as severe as they might have been. The focus was more physical and material, less mental. The Querent may feel drained by her family or friends in her home town. She needs a new path for her energy which could be more satisfying.

12. Illusions regarding question. Secret enemies:
Page of Wands reversed
This is a young person in the Querent's environment who doesn't want to work. They may be lazy and dishonest also. It could mean that the Querent does not wish to continue working—that she would prefer to be free to come and go as she desires. She does love to travel and plans to do so in the future.

13. Future plans: 3 of Pentacles reversed
The Querent knows she is good at her job but feels that she is underpaid. Her employer allows her to take several trips during the year and the Querent feels guilty about asking for a raise. The situation is detrimental to the Querent's health.

14. Past emotional concerns: Ace of Cups

The Querent lost her husband three years ago and this has been a stressful emotional experience. Her dilemma is: her family in California have asked her to move there permanently but she has a son and daughter-in-law at home. There are new beginnings in love and emotions in California due to the imminent arrival of a new grandchild. The question is: "What to do?"

15. Goals for the Future: 9 of Swords

This is the crisis card. The Querent is feeling depressed because she knows that no matter what she does someone is going to be unhappy.

16. Goals for the Future: Queen of Pentacles reversed

The Querent fears she will be unable to earn money in the future and will become dependent on her family.

17. Goals for the Future: Ace of Pentacles reversed

No new beginnings with money. The Querent definitely has feelings of insecurity. Her decision to move to California will be based on her feelings of financial security. She will also consider her grandchildren because she truly loves them.

Summary

The Querent has a problem common to parents whose children have grown up, married and moved to another state. The difficulty for older people is making a new life and new friends in the new location. Another factor is being a widow(er). This can put a strain on the family to find things of interest for their parent. The Querent is very creative and until she makes her decision she could find work to do in her own home. This will give her funds for her trips and the freedom to come and go as she pleases.

The Querent must stop worrying and concentrate on what she truly desires to do with her life. This way she stays healthy and lives to a ripe old age (Capricorn). She can also be of service to her grandchildren and help them become productive and successful.

THE SEVEN CARD SPREAD

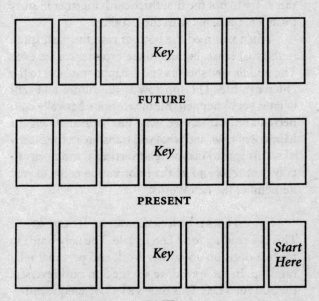

Key

FUTURE

Key

PRESENT

Key   *Start Here*

PAST

Have the Querent shuffle the cards and return them to you. Lay the cards out beginning with the bottom row, the past. Start on the right side and go to the left. Next add the second and third rows. Now look at the cards for repeat themes. Read the Key Words of each card first and then try to connect them in a story. This may seem difficult as you begin but it will get easier as you gain more confidence.

This reading begins on the right side and goes to the left. The middle card in each row is called the "Key." This card can be instrumental in making a decision between the first three cards and the last three. Try to put the first three cards together in story form. Do the same with the last three.

When you read the bottom row, the past, speak in the past tense, because these experiences are over. The middle row shows what is happening now in the Querent's life. The top row is the future and tells what is yet to happen. All the rows are basically connected and you can see what has happened, what is happening now, and what will transpire in the future.

This spread can be read vertically and horizontally. Just relax and let the information come to you. Remember the Key Words!

Seven Card Spread Sample Reading
This is a reading for a Leo female. The lady wants to make a decision about her work and personal relationship. In the spread we see the Sun card reversed; the Sun rules Leo. This shows a lack of energy, enthusiasm, joy, and honesty.

There are five Major Arcana and two Court cards. One third of the spread deals with other people and their influence in this lady's life. There are only three Cup cards, which means that love is not the focus nor are her emotions involved. The following cards were in the Querent's reading:

Past: Page of Wands rev., Empress rev., 6 of Pentacles rev., Ace of Wands, Hierophant, 9 of Swords, Hermit rev.

Page of Wands rev.: The Querent felt a lack of freedom. Her desire was to be able to do whatever she pleased, but she felt frustrated at work and/or in her social life.

Empress rev.: The Querent did not feel creative in the past. She had lost a child and was not fully recovered. She was unhappy about her failed marriage also.

6 of Pentacles rev.: During her marriage her choices regarding money were limited. Her relationship was not built on stable financial grounds. She had to allow others to make decisions for her.

Ace of Wands (Key): New beginnings in work and social activities diverted her attention. New people came into her life and she changed her direction. She made new decisions and divorced her husband.

Hierophant: The Querent believed in her relationship. She had faith that her marriage and pregnancy would work out fine. She accepted her experiences regardless of the circumstances.

9 of Swords: Then came the crisis period. She was very depressed and didn't know what to do. Everything seemed so black. The Querent lost the baby at this time. Her husband offered her little comfort.

The Hermit rev.: The Querent did not seek help within. She had closed her mind at that point and did not use the wisdom she had gained through her experiences. The help she did get was for her mate, who did not listen.

Present: *6 of Wands rev., King of Swords, Ace of Cups, Sun rev., 3 of Swords, 7 of Swords, 10 of Pentacles rev.*

6 of Wands rev.: The decisions the Querent is making are not positive. There is no victory in the work or social activities. She may be waiting for others to make the decisions that affect her life

King of Swords: This card refers to a Gemini male, a lawyer or someone in authority. The Querent's employer is a Libra, an air sign, which is the same element as Gemini. This person is mentally capable of helping the Querent.

Ace of Cups: New beginnings in love or an emotional involvement. A new relationship or a move to a new home. The Querent is more balanced and peaceful at this time. She may be using her intuition now.

The Sun rev. (Key): The Querent has low energy at this time. She is feeling a lack of new ideas which halts her creative flow. There could be a fear of limitation in her relationships or at work. The Querent needs ego strokes and approval to do her best work. Without the attention and applause she becomes depressed.

3 of Swords: The Querent is making her own problems and troubles. There is a three-way conflict, jealousy and pettiness in her surroundings. She feels she is being stabbed in the back by coworkers. There is some cheating and dishonesty also.

7 of Swords: The Querent is trying to control her path by mental means. She is in a temporary situation. There is a desire for a new relationship now, but she fears hurting her current boyfriend. She must let go of old habits for new growth.

10 of Pentacles rev.: There will be no changes in the Querent's finances. Her money will not come through an inheritance or gambling. Her sources of income will continue through her work.

Future: *2 of Pentacles rev., 3 of Cups, Queen of Swords rev., 5 of Wands, 5 of Cups, 6 of Swords, Magician*

2 of Pentacles rev.: The Querent is a spendthrift; she has problems managing her money. She feels she can always work and make whatever money she needs. Leo people are usually very generous. This Leo is no exception, it seems from her conversation.

3 of Cups: The Querent desires to be happy, creative and free to travel in her work. She enjoys going to parties, dinner and theater. Invitations to happy events are coming to her soon. She may hope to marry again and have other children.

Queen of Swords rev.: The Querent does not wish to be single. Her creative drives are for work and pleasure, including sex. She needs a relationship (positive or not). This card refers to a Libra female (negative) or a Libra man. Her employer is a Libra man.

5 of Cups: The Querent is a romantic and believes in love. She maintains her faith by getting involved in relationships, positive or negative. This card suggests "crying over spilled milk." The Querent is still affected by her past experiences, which she must release.

6 of Swords: The Querent must now make choices regarding her problems and troubles. She can stay and face them or run away. Perhaps she is deciding to take a trip around water in the near future.

The Magician: This is the last card in the row and is very important. This card tells the Querent that there are many new beginnings for her, also many new directions she can take. She needs to meditate and ask for guidance in both her personal and public life.

5 of Wands (Key): The Querent believes in her work and social life. She wants to have things her way due to her ego needs. Her coworkers desire their way in the work and this can create much dissension. The Querent will find that life is constant change and everyone gets a chance to be a star.

Summary: There are many Swords in this spread which can mean potential health problems for the Querent. Being a Leo, this lady is a strong and determined type, who prefers that others do not see her weaknesses. She is independent and fears dependency. A relationship is based on a balance between independence and dependence. Old habit patterns which have her attracting the same sort of relationships must be changed. She can do this through meditation and the desire to change her life.

The Querent must be honest in all her dealings especially in relationships. She needs to make up her mind about what she truly wants in her life and go for it! This will improve her health and vitality. Leos enjoy good times, being around children, and using their creativity. This Leo fits that pattern.

THE HOROSCOPE SPREAD

The Querent shuffles the cards and hands them to the reader. While the Querent is shuffling, he makes a wish and also thinks of the question(s) he would like answered. The reader begins by placing a card, face up, in the first or Aries House and then continues around the horoscope, placing a card in each of the twelve houses. Remember the Key Words of each card and apply them as they relate to that particular house.

A. One can begin the reading at the birth sign of the Querent and continue around the zodiac wheel explaining the potentials through each card. This shows events in the past, present, and future.

B. One can begin in the present month and continue around the twelve houses. This projects most experiences into the future. The present month shows events now taking place.

If the cards speak of negative events, the Querent has the opportunity to change circumstances through awareness. This information is important to the seeker and is the reason for the reading. Complete the session in a positive manner. This helps the person feel competent to withstand any negative effects the Tarot information has brought to the self-conscious mind.

Aries (March 21-April 20)
Taurus (April 21-May 21)
Gemini (May 22-June 21)
Cancer (June 22-July 23)
Leo (July 24-August 23)
Virgo (August 24 - September 23)
Libra (September 24-October 23)
Scorpio (October 24-November 22)
Sagittarius (November 23-December 21)
Capricorn (December 22-January 20)
Aquarius (January 21-February 19)
Pisces (February 20-March 20)

1st House: Personality, Self
2nd House: Money, self-worth, possessions
3rd House: Siblings, neighbors. lower mind, trips
4th House: Home issues, mother, real estate
5th House: Love, pride, children, gambling, creativity
6th House: Work and health, servants
7th House: Relationships, legal matters, marriage
8th House: Sex, money, insurance, transformation
9th House: Truth, religion, higher philosophy, travel
10th House: Career, social standing, father, honor
11th House: Friends, hopes, wishes
12th House: Creativity, psychic ability, enemies, illusion

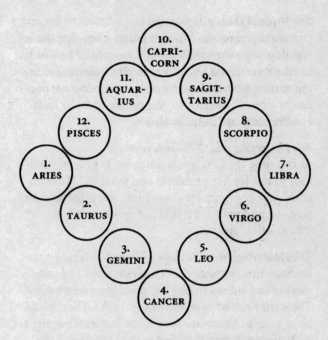

HOROSCOPE SPREAD SAMPLE READING

This is a young lady in her late thirties. She is a Libra, never married, lives alone, and supports herself. She has a dog as her companion whom she adores. The reading began in the 7th House or Libra. This is the house of: marriage, relationships, justice, equality, and open enemies.

There are five cards (Swords) in the layout, which can indicate health problems. There are four Major Arcana and five Court cards meaning many people have influence (positive or negative) in her life.

7th House/Libra: 4 of Swords
During this time the Querent must realize that she is creating her own problems and troubles. She needs to take time to rest and put herself in balance. Learning to have faith and overcoming ego desires are necessary now. "Don't burn the candle at both ends." Health issues are in focus also.

8th House/Scorpio: 7 Swords reversed
At this time the Querent is not using her mental abilities to resolve her problems and troubles. This situation may continue for some time. She is focused on physical and material needs not spiritual values. Her inner faith is lacking.

9th House/Sagittarius: Page of Swords reversed
During this period the Querent may feel more mature and willing to face her problems and troubles. These may not be as severe as she thinks. There could be a young Aquarian person in her environment with problems and this person may need her help.

10th House/Capricorn: The Fool
During this month the Querent will be looking for new experiences and adventures. She may not pay too much attention to what is going on around her. She could make changes in her work or home but should investigate her motives for doing so.

11th House/Aquarius: The Hermit reversed
During this month the Querent will not be open-minded nor will she use wisdom earned through her experiences. She may get in touch with old friends

because she does not wish to be alone. She must learn to be less judgmental and to relax and enjoy life.

12th House/Pisces: King of Swords reversed

The Querent has a legal suit pending and is dissatisfied with her lawyer. During this period she may find a new lawyer if she has not done so. This card signifies a Gemini man who is not positive, or a lawyer who is not doing a good job. It could also indicate a Gemini woman coming into the Querent's life.

1st House/Aries: The Sun reversed

At this time the Querent may not feel very energetic. She may not be as open or honest as she could be. Her expectations may not reach the level she desires, and her ego will be unhappy. Perhaps there is something the Querent is afraid of which could concern her health also. Low self-esteem.

2nd House/Taurus: Knight of Swords

During this month the Querent will receive news of problems and troubles. The news will not be positive. The problems can come from family members or friends and will involve money. (The 2nd House refers to money, possessions, and self-worth.) The person with the troubles can be an Aquarian.

3rd House/Gemini: 4 of wands

This card is very positive. During this month the work and home situation will be fruitful and happy. The Querent may decide to buy a home, there could be a marriage in the family or she could get a raise or new job. Experiences are favorable.

4th House/Cancer: Queen of Wands

During this period the Querent will be interested in gaining recognition and ego satisfaction. Home issues and real estate needs are important. She could even work from the home. Potential for promotion.

5th House/Leo: King of Wands reversed

An Aries person (or Aries type) is in the Querent's environment. If it is a male, he is immature, egotistical, and self-centered. If it is a female, she could be a friend who enjoys going places and doing things with the Querent. At this time there is a need to initiate actions and use will power at work or home.

6th House/Virgo: The Tower reversed

The Querent refuses to give up old habit patterns and problems are brewing. Catastrophic events are potentials for the future. The Querent must think positively about her old experiences or early traumas and release old negative thoughts. She also must pay attention to her work especially at this time.

Summary

The Querent has several options in her future. The cards show the potential for more money, a better position at work, and a different home. There are several cards that indicate negative thinking that must be changed. Health and diet must also be a focus. The only way to change our lives is to change our thinking.

This spread shows potentials for the future. To be in touch with this information gives the Querent the ability to make changes now and change her future in the process.

THE TREE OF LIFE SPREAD

1. LIGHT

Outcome

3. UNDER-STANDING

Receptivity, Limitations, Creativity

2. WISDOM

Power, Goals, Changes

5. SEVERITY STRENGTH

Activity, Destruction, Struggle

6. BEAUTY

New insights, Compassion, Love

4. MERCY

Memories, Abundance, Generosity

8. GLORY

Discrimination, Analysis, Knowledge

9. FOUNDA-TION

Subconscious fears, Illusions, Sexual focus

7. VICTORY

Desires, Emotions, Romance

10. KINGDOM

Practicality, Money, Physical possession

The Tree of Life reading can be done with just the Major Arcana cards. Do the spread with all 78 cards or just the Majors and decide which you prefer. Remember to tell the Querent (person receiving the reading) to make a wish while shuffling the cards.

After the cards are returned to you, begin laying them out starting from number ten and ending on number one. Every sphere has its own explanation. These examples should give you, the reader, an idea of how to read this spread. The Tree of Life spread covers many areas and has the potential to answer any or all questions.

Example:

Ace of Cups on sphere 1: New beginnings in love and emotions. Some Light concerning the will.

Hierophant reversed on sphere 9: Refusing to believe in subconscious fears or illusions. The focus is not sexual and may be spiritual.

Strength reversed on sphere 7: Not having the Strength to overcome desires, too emotional and romantic. Little Victory.

Two of Cups on sphere 2: Through Wisdom, I know my love and emotions are healthy.

The Hermit reversed on sphere 8: There is no Glory in a closed mind. Person does not use discrimination, try to analyze the situation or seek knowledge.

The Tree of Life Sample Reading

This is a reading for a young man whose question concerns a book he is writing. He would like to know if it will be published.

Glancing over the cards we see that the young man has a very positive outlook overall. There are three Major Arcana and two Court cards. Half the spread relates to people or ideas in the Querent's head. If these cards refer to people perhaps this indicates interference or influence being exerted over the young man, positive or negative.

The cards in the spread are as follows:

10th Position/Kingdom: 8 of Pentacles

The Querent has the strength to learn a new skill and create a new ego personality. The Kingdom is his environment, which includes people, money, practicality, and physical possessions. He may not be earning large sums of money now but he enjoys his work and the people in his surroundings. The Querent is strong enough to become successful using his creative abilities.

9th Position/Foundation: 4 of Pentacles

The Querent realizes his potential for making money. The Foundation includes subconscious fears, illusions, and sexual needs. The Querent may be too focused on making money and forgetting the purpose of writing the book. Due to early fears in his life he may be greedy for financial security. There is also a potential for investing in real estate.

8th Position/Glory or Splendor: 4 of Cups

The Querent must understand that past experiences can block his current thoughts and deny him success. The Glory for the Querent will be when he realizes his old habit patterns regarding his love and emotions. Discrimination, maintaining a balance, and paying attention to his associations will be to his advantage. New opportunities are there for him.

7th Position/Victory: Ace of Wands

New beginnings in work and social activities bring Victory. The Querent was bored with his routine and desired a new direction. He is creative and decided to become a writer. There could be some invitations of a social nature in the near future.

6th Position/Beauty: The Hanged Man

The Beauty of this sphere is love from the heart Through meditation, quieting the mind and getting in touch with his inner teacher, the Querent could be led to fame and fortune! Without love, the Querent may never finish the book or reap his reward.

5th Position/Strength: Page of Swords

This card refers to an Aquarian who is bringing messages of problems and troubles to the Querent. The Aquarian is a young man or woman and could be the Querent's friend who needs help. He has the strength to cope with these problems (the Querent). He also must learn to balance his energies and be aware of his ego focus and desires.

4th Position/Mercy: Queen of Pentacles

The Queen of Pentacles refers to work and health issues. This Queen is a Virgo and can be too critical or too much of a perfectionist. This sphere includes memories, generosity, and abundance. The Querent may have past memories regarding a lack of abundance or little generosity from the females in his family. This card can signify mother, sister, or other women in his life. There is a need for mercy in his relationships with everyone.

3rd Position/Understanding: The High Priestess

The High Priestess says "I know all things." The Querent understands his limitations but he also knows his creative abilities. The Querent is receptive to information that will aid him on his way to success. The Moon rules the High Priestess, which again refers to memories and the subconscious mind. The seed ideas are in the Querent's mind and can be used as material for the book.

2nd Position/Wisdom: 8 of Cups reversed

The Querent is not using wisdom through his experiences in positive ways. He is undergoing an emotional drain due to a loss or separation. The Querent feels he must pursue his relationships whether he has the strength to do so or not. He has set a goal for himself which he thinks will afford him the necessary changes that will make his life successful.

1st Position/Light (outcome): The Star

This card is extremely positive as the outcome. The Querent must keep his eyes on the goal at all times. Through meditation his inner teacher will guide him and provide the Light on his creative path. This will enable the Querent to finish his book, get it published, and out to the public.

Summary

The Querent is being told that he can find success through his writing abilities. Meditation is a key (Hanged Man and Star cards). The High Priestess suggests intelligence; therefore, the book will be well received by the public. This is a very positive spread and promises ultimate victory for the Querent.

Symbols: Tools for Understanding

The symbols listed here are a compilation from many sources. They have been assembled over a long period of time, through many books on Tarot, Cabalah, Astrology, and other books related to metaphysics. As we come into life we accept the conditions surrounding us and ask no questions regarding what we see. Everything is taken for granted and the meanings behind what we encounter do not penetrate our thinking.

In the past, the symbol of a vertical line represented man. Man began to count through this symbol also. The second step in man's progression was the horizontal line. This line portrayed woman and was taken from a representation of the Moon. The Moon reposing on her back shows her receptivity; the vertical line was considered projective and phallic. When these two lines are crossed equally they indicate the four elements in balance. This symbol is shown on the High Priestess, Key 2 and suggests that her heart is in balance. The five-pointed star or pentagram is a sign of man. The top point is the head, the two horizontal points are the arms and the bottom points refer to the feet. This symbol also indicates balance and when reversed refers to black magic or wrong use of positive energy. The six-pointed star or Star of David contains the upright triangle representing fire (sexual energy). The down-pointing triangle is a water symbol indicating emotions, intuition, and subconsciousness.

SYMBOLS

All of these symbols are connected to the four elements: fire air, earth, and water. None of these symbols began as religious emblems. They have been used by initiates and great teachers of all ages to represent certain spiritual truths which the average person could not understand. These symbols describe hidden or "occult" knowledge. One of the reasons we hear the phrase "man is asleep" is due to the acceptance of this symbolic world without questioning its source or meaning. The Tarot is a valuable aid in awakening us to Truth. Not everyone using the cards will penetrate the deeper meanings, but for those who desire the knowledge or whose interests go beyond the surface of life the Tarot is a major step forward. The symbols are contained within each of us, as C. G. Jung declared in his many writings on the Collective Unconscious.

A.

Above: upper brain, pineal gland

Abyss: pitfall, chaos, womb of the earth, subconscious

Adam: humanity, spirit, earth life, red clay

Air: spirit, light, mind

Akasha: race memories, record of experiences, karma

Angel: divine breath, spiritual ideas, messengers

Animals: emotions, desires, five senses

Ankh: life, immortality, union of heaven and earth; with eagle—freedom from bondage

Arbor: shelter built from nature

Archangels:
  Raphael: (Key 6) God as healer (charity)
  Michael: (Key 14) Sun God (Holiness)
  Gabriel: (Key 20) calls to God (strength)

Arrow: phallic, directed will, vengeance

Aura: force field surrounding the body, electricity, colors designate health conditions

B.

Babel: (Key 16) house (body) built on words, language, lost word of God

Banner:
  white banner and red cross: innocence and blood
  held in right hand: conscious awareness
  held in left hand: automatic reactions

Battlements: (Key 18) gateway to beyond, not the final boundary

Bee: royalty, industry, order, sociability

Belt: time, limitation

Bird: freedom, messengers, telepathy

Blindfold: inner vision, not focused on materialism

Body: temple or kingdom of God, tabernacle

Book: Torah, record of Truth, measure of time, memories, akasha

Bread: life substance, flesh, the body

Breath: (Key 0) life, ego, solar/lunar energies, inspiration, spirit

Butterfly: immortality, rebirth, soul

C.

Caduceus: kundalini, moral balance, healing energies, two entwined serpents indicate sickness and health

Candlestick: spine, seven candles—the chakras

Canopy: celestial influence, protection, mind

Cat: astral world, power of darkness, good eyesight, nine lives (nine is the number of completion)

Chosen People: spiritually enlightened humanity

Christ: the heart, the Higher Self, cosmic truth, spirit

Circle: eternity, cycles of manifestation, perfection

City: thought centers

Clouds: human thoughts in discord, storm clouds indicate unwise thinking

Colors:

  black: negative, passive, ignorance, female

  blue: intuition, peace, life

  gold: soul power, enlightenment

  green: desire, healing, growth

  gray: harmony, balance of opposites

  indigo: devotion, peace

  red: energy, courage, vitality, passion, action

  silver: mystical, magnetic

  white: purity, truth, perfection

  yellow: intellect, knowledge

Crayfish: (Key 18) early stages of unfolding, unconscious mind

Cross: four elements, masculine/feminine polarity, matter
   solar cross: balanced energies
   triple cross: divine, intellectual and physical world,
   generative power
Cube: physical world
Cherubim: sacred wisdom

D.

Dancer: (Key 21) victory over the elements, rhythm,
   attainment
Desert: barren thoughts, seeming lack of substance or life
Devil: false concepts of the physical world
Dog: fidelity, guardian
Dolphin: ancient friend of man
Door: threshold, portal, entrance to the temple
Dove: Holy Spirit, peace, bird of Venus

E.

Eagle: hope, aspiration, higher thought power
   two-headed eagle: omnipotence
East: interior, within, hidden
Eden: solar plexus, Paradise
Egg: seed forms, ideas
Elements: fire, air, earth, water
Ether: life substance, fifth element, quintessence
Eve: soul, feeling, feminine principle, receptivity
Eye: (Third) organ of true spiritual vision
Evil: missing the mark, errors in thinking

F.

Feather: eagle, Scorpio
Feet: comprehension, support, progress
Fence: limitation
Field: body, substance
Fish: ideas, increase

Fixed signs: fixed conditions on earth or in mind
Flowers: vegetable kingdom, reproductive organs
Flying creatures: mental thoughts, telepathy, messengers
Frankincense: love, consecration, spirituality

G.

Gabriel: strength of God
Garden: subconsciousness, solar plexus, substance, earth
Garland: fruitfulness, festivities
Gentiles: worldly thoughts
Girdle: time, spiritual force
Globe: universe, cosmic egg
   winged globe: exultation, transcendence, knowledge
Gnosis: knowledge
Grapes: fertility, abundance, life

H.

Halo: spiritual force, auric egg
Head: place of the intellect, crown
Heart: love, emotions, seat of judgment,
   pierced: wounded love or emotions, pain
Heights: spiritual ascendancy
Hermit: Higher Self, inner teacher
Horns: strength, penetrating
Horse: progress, vitality, five senses, fertility
   winged horse: solar power, intellect

I.

Ibis: immortal life, vigilance
Ice: frozen mental attitude
Ideas: seed thoughts
Iris: healing, love

J.

Jackal: animal kingdom, sharp eyes, keen sense of smell

Jewels: wisdom and love

Jews: religious thoughts

K.

Keys: opens the mysteries

    gold: self conscious activity (solar)

    silver: subconscious emotions (lunar)

King: the will

Kundalini: serpent fire, seven chakras rising up spine

L.

Ladder: roadway of the gods, leading to perfection, kundalini

Lame: disabled thoughts, lacking understanding or progress

Lamp: light center in the heart

Lantern: search for truth, light of the intellect

Lead: metal of Saturn, labor, responsibility

Leaves: growth, vitality

Lemniscate (figure eight on side): path of discipleship, eternity

Lightning flash: truth, reality, inspiration

Lingan and Yoni: procreation, male/female, sexual symbol

Lion: fire element, desire body, action

    red lion: animal reproductive force, passion

    green lion: animal nature, impure

Lotus: purity, divine knowledge, mystic center, crown chakra

M.

Maya: illusion regarding the world

Metals: gold, silver, mercury, lead, copper, tin, iron— these refer to the planets also

Mirror: reflection, judgment

Moon center: pituitary gland, cycles, memory

Mountain: abstract thought, attainment, realization, path to the heights

N.

Natural man: a seed of what man can become spiritually

North: hidden, darkness, unknown, ignorance

Nude: innocence, truth, free of dogma

O.

Oil: prana, love, vital fluid, illumination

Olive oil: Holy Spirit, peace, love

Owl: wisdom, a familiar of Merlin the magician

Ox-bull: generative force, strong, patient, self-sacrificing, forever toiling

P.

Palm: victory over death

Path: attainment, states of becoming, steps to the heights

Pearls: wisdom (pearls of great price)

Pelican: sacrifice, mother love

Pentagram (five-pointed star): mental dominion, figure of man, five relates to the Hierophant

Phoenix (highest state of Scorpio): grace, rising from the ashes of experience

Planets: interior stars or chakras

Pomegranate: fertility, female seeds, death/resurrection

Pool: female symbol, womb, substance, receptivity

R.

Rainbow: protection, good fortune, perfection (seven rays)

Ram: physically strong, assertive, a noble beast

Reptiles: sexual will, action, kundalini

River: currents of thought or vital forces, the blood

Rod: discipline, mastery, phallus
   flowering rod: virility

ROTA: wheel, karma, royal road
S.
Salamander: fire elemental
Salt: earth, preservative, inertia, resurrection
Scales: equilibrium, weighing justice
Scarab: immortality, self existent being
Scepter: wisdom, royalty, dominion
Scorpion: immortality, treachery, danger
Scroll: hidden mysteries, akasha
Sea: universal principle, all potentials
Serpent: sense consciousness, desire, tempter, wisdom
   uplifted or coiled on cross: regeneration, salvation
Seven: natural man, cycles of time, periods of growth,
   planets, chakras
Sheep: innocence, purity
   lamb: loving, intellect, obedience
Shellfish: insulated, protective, ideas
Ship: sanctuary, body, activity
Sphere: creative motion, rotation, cyclic
Sphinx: guardian of the temple, ancient occult wisdom,
   holds the riddle of human existence
Spiral: rising in consciousness, kundalini force
Square: earth, foundation, materiality, limitation
Staff or rod: sign of power
   uplifted: creative power of the mind
Stairs: rising to a higher state of consciousness
Stars: spirit, guiding light, truth
   five-pointed: Star of the Magi, symbol of man
   six-pointed: Shield of Solomon, magical power, union
     of the elements, human soul perfected
   seven-pointed: spirituality, mysticism, wisdom
Stone: conscious union with Truth on physical plane

Stream: subconsciousness, thought currents, river of life
Sulfur: passion, desire, hell, devil, red lion
Swan: royalty, initiation
Sword: mind, protection, knowledge
   upright: truth
   two-edged: the tongue
Sylphs: air spirits

T.

Tabernacle: body, transitory, a state of consciousness
Tares: negative error thoughts
Tau: salvation, eternal life, Hebrew
Temple: body, house of God
Ten: completion, perfection, beginning new cycle
Tent: transitory building, temporary structure (body)
Third eye: golden flower, the stone, clairvoyance
Thorns: pain, martyrdom
Threshold: crossing, entering new way
Throat: speech, Venus center, desire, Hierophant
Thumbs: will, executive ability
Thunderbolt: celestial fire, Jove, lightning flash
Tomb: body, materiality,
Tower: personality, human thoughts, speech, false ideas
Trees: nerves, regeneration, sheltering, nourishing, spine
   evergreen: everlasting
   fir: nobility, elevation
   oak: honor, strength, integrity
   olive: passion
   palm: help, healing, victory
   pine: humanities
   Tree of Knowledge: understanding of good and evil,
     discernment, free will, separation from God, feminine
   Tree of Life: absolute life principle, roots centered in

solar plexus, nerves, spinal column, masculine

Trefoils: (on Fool's garment) the Trinity

Trumpet: power of sound

Twelve: spiritual number of fulfillment, important nerve centers in the body, tribes of Israel, sons of Jacob, disciples of Jesus, signs of the Zodiac, man's spiritual faculties

Triangle:
    pointed up: fire air
    pointed down: water earth

Typhon: evil monster, darkness

U.

Undine: water spirits

Unicorn: mystery, allegory of Christ, innocence, moral purity

Urns:
    silver urns: soul, feminine
    gold urns: spirit, masculine, life fluid

Urim and Thummin: lights, truth, perfection, revelation

V.

Valley: subconsciousness, field of experience, life

Vases: womb, transformation, astral fluid

Veil: cover for hidden mysteries, virginity

Vine: life, abundance, wisdom
    grapevine: nervous system

Voice: power of the spoken word or Logos

W.

Wall: limitation (manmade)

Wallet: tools, memory, abilities, talents

Water: cleansing, astral fluid, universal substance, subconsciousness

Waterfall: male potency, phallic symbol

Water pots: nerve centers filled with the water of life
West: solar plexus, past
Wheat: abundance, fertility, fruitfulness
  wheat from chaff: separating truth from falsehood
Wheel: cycles, chakras
  eight-spoked wheel: spirit,
Widow: half truths, belief in lack or separation
Wilderness: transitory state, undisciplined and unculti-
  vated thoughts
Wine: vitality between soul and body, spirit, life
Wings: freedom from material limitations
Wolf: destructive untamed consciousness
Worlds: Archetypal (the Ideal), Creative, Formative,
  Matter (Earth)
Wreath: victory, praise, attainment, spiritual force of
  nature

Y.

Y: three paths, three in one
Yods: falling drops of light, dew from heaven, descent of
  spirit
Yoke: yoga, two paths (male/female)

Z.

Z: lightning flash, sudden knowledge
Zero: infinity, eternity, source of All
Zodiac: cycles of existence, characteristics of humanity

There are many more source books for discovering the meanings of symbols. The search for this information is very rewarding for those sincere seekers. It is said "seek and ye shall find." Following is a list of books which have additional information concerning symbols:

Secret Teachings of All Ages by Manly P. Hall
A Dictionary of Symbols by J. Cirlot
Meditation and the Kabbalah by Aryeh Kaplan
The Mystical Qabalah by Dion Fortune
Ancient Myths by Rudolph Steiner
The Royal Road by Stephan Hoeller
Cosmic Consciousness by R. M. Bucke
Symbols and the Symbolic by de Lu Bicz
The Black Arts by Richard Cavendish
Illustrations of Masonry by William Preston
Book of Thoth by Aleister Crowley
Hidden Wisdom in the Bible by Geoffrey Hodson
Jung and Tarot by S. Nichols
The Qabalistic Tarot by Robert Wang
The Source of Measure by J. Ralston Skinner

BIBLIOGRAPHY

Campbell and Roberts. *Tarot Revelations*

Case, Paul F. *Highlights of Tarot, Book of Tokens*

Connolly, E. *Tarot Vol. I: Handbook for the Apprentice; Tarot Vol. II: Handbook for the Journeyman*

Crowley, Aleister. *The Book of Thoth*

Douglas, A. *Tarot, Origins, Meanings and Uses of the Cards*

Fortune, Dion. *The Mystical Qabalah*

Franck, A. *Kabbalah*

Gray, Eden. *Complete Guide to the Tarot*

Greer, Mary. *Tarot Mirrors*

Halevi, B. *Adam and the Kabbalistic Tree*

Hoeller, Stephan. *The Royal Road*

Kaplan, Aryeh. *Meditation and the Kabbalah*

Mathers, S. L. MacGregor. *The Tarot*

Maxwell, Joseph. *The Tarot*

Nichols, S. *Jung and Tarot*

Ouspensky, P. D. *Symbolism of the Tarot*

Papus. *Tarot of the Bohemians*

Poncé, Charles. *Kabbalah*

Sadhu, Mouni. *The Tarot*

Waite, Arthur E. *The Pictorial Key to the Tarot*

Wang, Robert. *Qabbalistic Tarot*

Wirth, Oswald. *The Tarot of the Magicians*

Zain, C. C. *Sacred Tarot*

ORDER LLEWELLYN BOOKS TODAY

Llewellyn publishes hundreds of books on your favorite subjects! To get these exciting books, including the ones on the follow pages, check your local bookstore or order them directly from Llewellyn.

Order Online:
Visit our website at www.llewellyn.com, select your books, and order them on our secure server.

Order by Phone:
- Call toll-free within the U.S. at 1-877-NEW-WRLD (1-877-639-9753). Call toll-free within Canada at 1-866-NEW-WRLD (1-866-639-9753)
- We accept VISA, MasterCard, and American Express

Order by Mail:
Send the full price of your order (MN residents add 7% sales tax) in U.S. funds, plus postage & handling to:

Llewellyn Worldwide
P.O. Box 64383, Dept. 1-56718-001-9
St. Paul, MN 55164-0383, U.S.A.

Postage & Handling:
Standard (U.S., Mexico, & Canada). If your order is:
Up to $25.00, add $3.50
$25.01 - $48.99, add $4.00
$49.00 and over, FREE STANDARD SHIPPING
(Continental U.S. orders ship UPS. AK, HI, PR, & P.O. Boxes ship USPS 1st class. Mex. & Can. ship PMB.)

International Orders:
Surface Mail: For orders of $20.00 or less, add $5 plus $1 per item ordered. For orders of $20.01 and over, add $6 plus $1 per item ordered.

Air Mail:
Books: Postage & Handling is equal to the total retail price of all books in the order.
Non-book items: Add $5 for each item.

Orders are processed within 2 business days. Please allow for norma shipping time. Postage and handling rates subject to change.

How to Use Tarot Spreads

Sylvia Abraham

Being a skilled tarot reader requires the ability to address the querent's specific concerns in a way that is understandable and memorable. Now, for the first time, there is a book of specific tarot spreads that will provide the answers to the most commonly asked questions about love and romance . . . home and family . . . business and finance . . . major life events such as marriage, pregnancy, and divorce . . . travel and relocating . . . inner fears and personal development . . . spiritual growth and past lives. A common problem for tarot readers is how to put the cards together so they make sense. It helps to be a good storyteller, to bring the cards to life in a dramatic way that stays with your querents long after they have gone home. The thirty-seven time-tested spreads in this book help you gain the confidence to do just that. You will also see real-life readings for each spread that were conducted by the author. Plus, *How To Use Tarot Spreads* includes the upright and reversed meanings of each card as well as the steps to conducting a positive tarot reading.

1-56718-002-7, 272 pp., illus. $5.99

Tarot for Beginners

P. Scott Hollander

The Tarot is much more than a simple divining tool. While it can—and does—give you accurate and detailed answers to your questions when used for fortunetelling, it can also lead you down the road to self-discovery in a way that few other meditation tools can do. *Tarot for Beginners* will tell you how to use the cards for meditation and self-enlightenment as well as for divination.

If you're just beginning a study of the Tarot, this book gives you a basic, straightforward definition of the meaning of each card that can be easily applied to *any* system of interpretation, with *any* Tarot deck, using *any* card layout. The main difference between this book and other books on the Tarot is that it's written in plain English—you need no prior knowledge of the Tarot or other arcane subjects to understand its mysteries, because this no-nonsense guide will make the symbolism of the Tarot completely accessible to you. You will receive an overview of of the cards of the Major and Minor Arcana in terms of their origin, purpose, and interpretive uses as well as clear, in-depth descriptions and interpretations of each card.

1-56718-363-8, 352 p., illus   **$12.95**